THE MAPLE SYRUP
COOKBOOK

40 Easy, Delicious & Healthy Maple Syrup Recipes
for Breakfast Lunch & Dinner

Jean Legrand

Other recipe books by Jean LeGrand:

The Maple Syrup Cookbook Volume 2
Romantic Treats
Mother's Day Recipes
FrankenFood Recipes #1
FrankenFood Recipes #2
Fruit Infused Water Recipes
Delicious & Healthy Paleo Recipes
Top Paleo Diet Recipes
Easter Brunch
Easter Dinner
Irish Treats
Irish Dinner
Irish Drinks

www.FastForwardPublishing.com

ISBN-13: 978-1503350182
ISBN-10: 1503350185

Table of Contents

A Gift for You

To say "Thank You" for buying *The Maple Syrup Cookbook,* we'd like to give you a copy of *Favorite Recipes*, a collection of 18 recipes for delicious and easy-to-prepare dishes from appetizers to baked goods to entrées to desserts.

Get Your Free Copy Here:

http://www.fastforwardpublishing.com/Thank-You-Favorite-Recipes.html

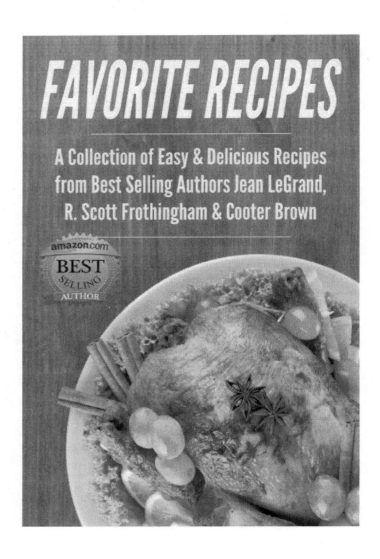

Introduction

Professional chefs and home cooks are discovering the taste and benefits of Maple Syrup beyond its traditional place in desserts and at the breakfast table. Used with a variety ingredients in a full list of cooking Instructions and styles, Maple Syrup is showing up as an ingredient in meals from lunch to dinner and from snacks to drinks.

For everyone -- from omnivore to vegan -- Maple Syrup offers a healthy alternative to sugar while imparting a pleasingly unique flavor to meals all around the world. I hope you enjoy this sampling of the exciting recipes that we have put together for this book.

Author's Note

I recently enjoyed an extended stay in Burlington, Vermont where Maple Syrup is a tradition that some Vermonters say is in their blood. They take their Maple Syrup seriously in Vermont and I feasted on many culinary offerings featuring that sweet, golden liquid treasure. Along with my childhood memories of Maple Syrup on pancakes and oatmeal, this visit inspired the writing of this book.

Every producer will vigorously defend his locale as the epicenter of Maple Syrup excellence. I'm not going to weigh in on who produces the best syrup (or maple sugar, or maple butter, or maple candy, etc.), but I will state that, for most purposes, I prefer the medium or dark amber Maple Syrup over the light amber. I guess that, in regards to Maple Syrup, I'm a grade B kind of guy. And, so as not to foment conflict between countries and states, regions and cities, towns and sugarhouses, that's as far as I'm willing to go in stating any kind of preference in regards to Maple Syrup.

All About Maple Syrup

What is Maple Syrup?

Maple syrup comes from the sap of maple trees. In the early spring, if you cut the bark or drill a hole into some species of maple trees, thin, clear sap (almost like water) will leak from the cut. This sap is about 2-percent sucrose and when boiled, the water evaporates, leaving maple syrup.

NOTE: Although some people tap the red maple and the silver maple, most will agree that the sap of the sugar (or rock) maple and the black maple produce the best syrup.

How is Maple Syrup Made?

When the sap of the maple tree flows in the late winter and early spring, it is collected for syrup making.

NOTE: Sap collection is best on days when the temperature is above freezing during the day and below freezing at night prior to bud formation. After the trees start to bud and produce leaves, the quality of the sap dramatically changes and cannot be used to produce syrup.

In the old days, a hole was drilled in the maple tree and a spout-like tap called a spile was inserted into the hole and a bucket was placed below the spile to collect the sap. These days, the sap is collected through plastic tubing

Once the sap has been collected, it is boiled down for hours in a special evaporator while it is monitored for viscosity and sugar density. Once boiled down, the syrup is filtered, graded and hot-packed (into sterile containers in a hot water bath).

Pure maple syrup is sold by shades of "amber." Although there are some different standards between states and countries that produce maple syrup, typically:

Light Amber has a fine, delicate flavor.

Medium Amber has a richer flavor and is most frequently used as table syrup.

Dark Amber is used for cooking, or as a table syrup by those who prefer a strong maple flavor.

Where is Maple Syrup Produced?

Because of specific weather conditions, maple syrup is only produced in the Northern part of North America, primarily in Quebec and Ontario in Canada and Maine, Massachusetts, Michigan, New Hampshire, New York, Ohio, Pennsylvania, Vermont, and Wisconsin in the United States.

NOTE: Quebec produces about three-quarters of the world's output

How Was Maple Syrup Discovered?

According to legend, one late-winter morning, Iroquois Chief Woksis, on his way to go hunting, pulled his tomahawk from the tree where he'd thrown it the night before. The weather was unseasonably warm and the tree's sap dripped from the gash made from the tomahawk and filled a container that was standing near the trunk. When the Chief's wife walked by the tree later, she thought container was plain water and cooked their evening meal in it. When boiled, the sap turned to syrup and the Chief liked the flavor. From that meal on, the Iroquois made and taught others to make maple syrup.

Can Maple Syrup be Substituted for Sugar in Recipes?

As a general rule of thumb, you can substitute one cup of maple granulated sugar for one cup of white sugar. Or, you can use one cup of maple syrup, but you'll also want to reduce any liquids in the recipe by approximately 3.7 ounces (between ⅓ cup and ½ cup) for each cup of sugar replaced.

NOTE: According to researchers at the International Maple Syrup Institute pure maple syrup delivers more overall nutritional value than many common sweeteners and has one of the lowest calorie levels while providing enhanced antioxidant levels. It may contain other health benefits that are currently being studied.

Is Maple Syrup a Healthy Choice?

When choosing between traditional sweeteners, pure Maple Syrup is a healthy option. Along with its sweetness and signature flavor, it also delivers beneficial vitamins, minerals and antioxidants.

Nutritional Value for Various Sweeteners
% of Recommended Daily Value (DV) per ¼ cup (60 ml)

	Maple Syrup	Corn Syrup	Honey	Brown Sugar	White Sugar
Manganese	95	0	4	2	0
Riboflavin	37	1	2	0	1
Zink	6	0	2	0	0
Magnesium	7	0	1	2	0
Calcium	5	0	0	4	0
Potassium	5	0	1	1	0
Calories	216	220	261	216	196

SOURCE: Canadian Nutrient File
(Health Canada) and USDA Nutrient Database

an LeGrand

Pure maple syrup is also very rich in antioxidants. It is reported that maple syrup has over 54 antioxidants that can help delay or prevent diseases caused by free radicals. The USDA database lists pure maple syrup on par or better than many vegetables when it comes to their antioxidant values.

Maple Syrup is also low on the Glycemic Index weighing in at (54) while white sugar is at (58) and honey is at (87). Experts agree that by consuming foods (55) or lower on the Glycemic Index can potentially help prevent or control diabetes, heart disease, and obesity.

Fun Facts About Maple Syrup

• It takes 30-50 gallons of sap to make one gallon of maple syrup.

• A maple that produces sap that can be made into maple sugar is called a sugarmaple.

• An area with a high concentration of sugarmaples is called a sugarbush.

• The building in which the maple syrup is produced is called a sugarhouse.

• The person who makes the maple syrup is called a sugarmaker.

• Native Americans were the first sugarmakers and they taught the Europeans all about the process.

• Maple syrup is boiled even further to produce maple cream, maple sugar, and maple candy.

• It takes one gallon of maple syrup to produce eight pounds of maple candy or sugar.

• A gallon of maple syrup weighs 11 pounds.

• The sugar content of sap averages 2.5 percent; sugar content of maple syrup is at 66 percent or more.

• Usually a maple tree is at least 30 years old and 12 inches in diameter before it is tapped.

• Tapping does no permanent damage and only 10 percent of the tree's sap is collected each year.

• Many maple trees have been tapped for 150 or more years.

• As the tree increases in diameter, more taps can be added - up to a maximum of four taps.

• Each tap will yield an average of 10 gallons of sap per season.

• The maple season may last eight to ten weeks, but sap flow is heaviest for about 10-20 days in the early spring (when the temperature is above freezing during the day and below freezing at night prior to bud formation).

The Syrup Used for the Recipes in this Book

All the recipes in this book use pure maple syrup: maple sap that has been collected and boiled down to obtain pure syrup without chemical agents or preservatives.

Do not confuse real maple syrup with "maple-flavored" syrups (also referred to as "pancake syrup", "waffle syrup", "table syrup", etc.) which are typically flavored high fructose corn syrup.

Strawberry Surprise Maple Oatmeal Muffins

12 servings

INGREDIENTS:

1 cup Greek yogurt

½ cup sliced strawberries

⅓ cup + 1 teaspoon maple syrup

2 cups gluten free oat flour

2 teaspoons baking powder

½ teaspoon Kosher salt

2 eggs

½ cup unsweetened applesauce

¼ cup almond milk

2 teaspoons vanilla extract

INSTRUCTIONS:

1. Preheat the oven to 350°F

2. Put liners into a 12 cup muffin pan

3. Put the yogurt, strawberries and 1 teaspoon of maple syrup in a blender and blend until smooth (about 2 minutes) and set aside

4. In a large mixing bowl, sift together the flour, baking powder and salt

5. In a medium-sized mixing bowl, stir together the ⅓ cup of maple syrup, eggs, applesauce, almond milk and vanilla extract until thoroughly combined

6. Pour the maple/eggs/applesauce/almond milk mixture over the flour/baking powder/salt mixture in the large mixing bowl and mix until all the ingredients are well combined

7. Add a small amount of the batter to the bottom of each muffin cup liner

8. Add a dollop of the yogurt/strawberry mixture from the blender on top of the batter in each muffin cut liner

9. Fill the muffin cups with more batter (over the until yogurt/strawberry mixture) until the cups are about ¾ of the way full.

10. Put the filled muffin pan onto the middle shelf in the oven and bake at 350°F for about 12-14 minutes.

11. Let the muffins cool completely before carefully removing them from the pan and serving

Maple Syrup Pecan Coffeecake

12 servings

INGREDIENTS:

~~192~~ ⁶ – Crumble Topping:

192 – 1½ cups all-purpose flour

1 cup pecans

146g ⅔ cup light brown sugar, packed

84g – 6 Tablespoons unsalted butter, softened

1½ teaspoon cinnamon

¼ teaspoon Kosher salt

¼ cup maple syrup

Cake:

256 – 2 cups all-purpose flour

1¼ teaspoon baking powder

¾ teaspoon baking soda

1 teaspoon Kosher salt

113g – ½ cup unsalted butter, softened

146g – ⅔ cup light brown sugar, packed

¼ cup maple syrup

1½ teaspoon maple extract

½ teaspoon vanilla extract

2 large eggs

¾ cup sour cream

INSTRUCTIONS:

Crumble Topping:

1. Put the flour, pecans, brown sugar, butter, cinnamon and salt into the bowl of food processor

2. Process until the pecans are ground and the mixture is crumbly

3. Add the maple syrup to the pecan/sugar/butter/cinnamon mixture and pulse until all ingredients are well combined

Cake:

1. Preheat the oven to 350°F

2. Butter and flour a 9-inch springform pan

3. In a small mixing bowl, whisk together the flour, baking powder, baking soda and salt

3. Using a standup mixer with a paddle attachment, cream the butter and brown sugar together until it is light and fluffy

4. Add the maple syrup, maple extract and vanilla to the butter/sugar mixture and mix well

5. One at a time, add the eggs to the maple/vanilla/butter/sugar mixture; beating after each addition

6. Add the sour cream to the egg/maple/vanilla/butter/sugar mixture and mix until just combined

7. Add the flour mixture to the sour cream/ egg/maple/vanilla/butter/sugar mixture and mix until just combined

8. Spread half the batter into the prepared springform pan

9. Sprinkle half of the crumb mixture evenly over the batter in the pan

10. Gently spread the remaining batter over the crumb mixture on the first half of the batter in the pan

11. Sprinkle the remaining crumb mixture over the batter in the pan

12. Transfer the filled pan to the center rack of the oven and bake at 350°F until a toothpick inserted into the center comes out clean (about 50-60 minutes)

13. Once the cake is cooked, remove it from the oven and let it cool in the pan on a cooling rack for the 5-10 minutes

14. After is has cooled, on a cooling remove the sides of the springform pan and let the cake continue to cool

15. Once the cake has cooled enough to be manageable, remove the bottom of the pan and let the cake cool completely on the cooling rack

16. Once completely cooled, transfer the cake to a serving place, and sprinkle the top lightly with confectioner's sugar just before serving.

Maple Granola

16 servings

INGREDIENTS:

    4 cups old-fashioned rolled oats

    1 cup shredded coconut (suggest unsweetened)

    1 cup sunflower seeds

    1 cup pumpkin seeds

    1 cup slivered almonds

    1 cup pecans, roughly chopped

    1 cup maple syrup

    ½ cup extra-virgin olive oil

    Kosher salt

    1 cup sweetened dried cranberries

INSTRUCTIONS:

1. Preheat the oven to 325°F

2. In a large mixing bowl, combine the rolled oats, coconut, sunflower seeds, pumpkin seeds, almonds, and pecans

3. Add the maple syrup and olive oil to the oats/coconut/seed/nut mixture and mix thoroughly

4. Sprinkle the syrup/oil/oats/coconut/seed/nut mixture with a generous pinch of salt

5. Spread the mixture onto large baking sheet, creating a uniform layer

6. Transfer the filled baking sheet to the oven and bake at 325°F, stirring every 15 minutes, until the granola is golden brown (about 1 hour)

7. Once cooled serve or store in an airtight container

Maple Syrup Breakfast Casserole

8 Servings

INGREDIENTS:

1 loaf (1 pound) French bread (day old works better than fresh)

1 package (8 ounce) cream cheese

2 cups milk

12 eggs

2 cups maple syrup plus more for serving

INSTRUCTIONS:

1. Grease a 9-inch x 13-inch baking dish

2. Slice the bread into about 25 slices

3. In a large mixing bowl, thoroughly whisk together the eggs, milk, and maple syrup

4. Place bread slices in the bottom of the prepared baking dish (until the bottom is covered)

5. Place about 2 teaspoons of cream cheese onto the center of each bread slice (don't spread the cheese)

6. Continue to layer with bread slices and cream cheese until the dish is filled

7. Carefully pour the egg mixture over the layers; don't let it run over the sides

8. Cover the filled baking dish with plastic wrap and refrigerate 8 hours (I just let it sit in the fridge overnight).

9. About an hour before you want to serve the casserole, bring the casserole out of the oven and preheat the oven to 375°F

10. Once the oven reaches 375°F, remove the plastic wrap and place the casserole on the center rack of the oven and bake until it is set and golden brown (about 45 minutes)

11. When fully cooked, remove the casserole from the oven and allow to cool in the pan for 5 minutes

12. Once slightly cooled, cut it into squares (or follow the shape of the bread slices) and serve with additional maple syrup

Maple Pecan Sticky Rolls

8 servings

INGREDIENTS:

Filling:

¾ cup dark brown sugar, packed

¼ cup granulated white sugar

¾ cup pecans, chopped

2 teaspoons cinnamon

⅛ teaspoon Kosher salt

1 tablespoon unsalted butter, melted

Dough:

3 cups all-purpose flour

3 tablespoons granulated white sugar

1 teaspoons baking powder

½ teaspoon baking soda

½ teaspoon Kosher salt

1 cup buttermilk

6 tablespoons unsalted butter, melted

⅓ cup maple syrup

Icing:

2 tablespoons unsalted butter, softened

3 tablespoons maple syrup

1 to 2 teaspoons milk

1 cup confectioners' sugar

INSTRUCTIONS:

1. In a small mixing bowl, combine the brown sugar, white sugar, pecans, cinnamon, and salt all of the dry ingredients in a small bowl

2. Add the melted butter to the sugar/pecan/spice mixture, stir with a fork until the mixture looks like wet sand and then set it aside

3. Preheat the oven to 425°F

4. Grease a 9-inch cake pan with butter

5. In a medium-sized bowl, sift together the flour, sugar, baking powder, baking soda, and salt

6. Add the buttermilk, syrup, and 2 tablespoons of the melted butter to the flour/sugar mixture, and stir until just combined

7. Transfer the flour/sugar/butter/syrup mixture to a floured work surface and knead until smooth

   NOTE: the dough will be soft and a little sticky

8. Put the dough in a lightly floured bowl, cover with plastic wrap, put the covered bowl, and chill for 20 minutes

9. Once chilled, on the floured surface, flatten the dough into a rectangle about 12 inches x 8 inches

10. Pour 2 tablespoons of the melted butter onto the dough rectangle and spread it around

11. Spread the filling evenly over the dough, leaving about a half inch border around the outside edge

12. Gently press the filling down, packing it on top of the dough

13. Starting on the long side of the dough, roll the side up, pressing as you go, to create a tightly rolled log

14. Pinch the seam of the roll closed and lay the "log" seam side down

15. Cut the log into 8 even pieces, and transfer each roll to the prepared cake pan, cut side up

16. Brush the rolls with the remaining 2 tablespoons of melted butter

17. Put the pan with the rolls onto the top shelf of the oven and bake at 425°F until the rolls are golden brown (about 20 to 25minutes)

18. When the rolls are properly cooked, remove them from the oven and allow them to cool for 5 minutes before icing

19. In a medium-sized mixing bowl, cream the butter until it is light and fluffy

20. Mix the sugar into the creamed butter

21. Whisk the maple syrup into the butter/sugar mixture until the mixture is smooth

> NOTE. If the icing is too thick, whisk in some milk, 1 teaspoon at a time, until you achieve the desired consistency

22. After the rolls have cooled in the pan for about 5 minutes, pour the icing over them and serve warm

Maple Butternut Squash & Apple Soup

8 servings

INGREDIENTS:

1 medium-sized butternut squash

2 teaspoons extra-virgin olive oil

2 Tablespoons maple syrup

Kosher and freshly ground black pepper

4 cloves of garlic, peeled, cut in half lengthwise

2 sprigs of thyme

2 baking apples, peeled, cored and quartered (I like the Jonathan, Red Rome, Courtland, and Crispin for baking)

4 cups chicken stock

INSTRUCTIONS:

1. Preheat oven to 375°F

2. Grease a rimmed baking sheet

3. Cut the squash in half lengthwise and remove the seeds

4. Brush the cut surfaces of squash and apples with maple syrup and then brush them again with the oil

5. Lightly season the apples with salt and pepper and then set them aside

6. Put garlic halves and a sprig of thyme in each squash half and then place them cut side down on the prepared baking sheet lace squash on a cookie sheet

7. Transfer the baking sheet with the squash to the center rack in the oven and bake at 375°F for 15 minutes

8. After baking the squash for 15 minutes, put the apples on the baking sheet with squash and continue baking at 375°F until the squash and apples are tender and soft (about 15-20 minutes more)

9. Once the squash and apples are properly cooked, remove them from the oven

10. Transfer the apples to a medium sauce pan

11. As soon as the squash is cool enough to handle, scrape the meat from the skin into the medium sauce pan with the apples (also put the cooked garlic into the pan - discard the squash skin and the thyme sprigs)

12. Mash the apples and squash with a potato masher

13. Add the chicken stock to the mashed apple/squash mixture (you can add all 4 cups of stock or less depending on the consistency of soup you like: less stock yields a thicker, heartier soup)

14. Turn heat to medium high under the saucepan with the apple/squash/stock mixture and heat, stirring constantly, until the soup comes to a boil

15. As soon as the soup begins to boil, turn off the heat

16. Taste the soup and add salt and pepper and maple syrup to your liking

17. Serve immediately

Maple Roasted Beet with Goat Cheese Salad

2 servings

INGREDIENTS:

6 small beets, peeled and quartered

1 tablespoon walnut oil

1 tablespoon maple syrup

pinch of Kosher salt

¼ pound lettuce

4 ounces goat cheese

2 Tablespoons sunflower seeds

Extra-virgin olive oil, for drizzling

INSTRUCTIONS:

1. Preheat oven to 425°F

2. Lightly grease a rimmed baking sheet

3. In a medium-sized mixing bowl, whisk together the oil, maple syrup, and salt

4. Toss the beets in the oil/syrup mixture and transfer them to the baking sheet

5. Put the baking sheet with the beets onto the center rack in the oven and roast 425°F at until soft and tender (about 45 minutes)

6. Once the beets are soft, remove them from the oven and toss them together with the lettuce, goat cheese, and sunflower seeds

7. Divide the beet/lettuce/cheese/seed mixture between two plates and drizzle with a touch of olive oil

8. Serve and enjoy

Maple Bacon and Cheese Sandwiches

4 servings

INGREDIENTS:

2 Tablespoons maple syrup

¼ Tablespoon water

1 Tablespoon Dijon mustard

2 Tablespoons lemon juice

⅛ teaspoon cayenne pepper

⅛ teaspoon ground cloves

2 whole wheat English muffins, split

1 pound bacon, sliced

1 large tomato, cut into thick slices

4 slices sharp cheddar cheese

INSTRUCTIONS:

1. Turn oven to broil

2. In a medium-sized mixing bowl, whisk together the maple syrup, water, mustard, lemon juice, pepper and cloves

3. In a large skillet, cook the bacon until it is cooked to your liking

4. Once the bacon is cooked to your liking, drain the far, add the maple/mustard/lemon/spice mixture to the skillet with the bacon, and cook for a few minutes to glaze the bacon

5. Remove the skillet with the bacon from the heat, add the tomatoes to the skillet (do not stir), and then set the skillet with the bacon, glaze and tomatoes aside

6. Put the muffin halves on a rimmed baking sheet and top with bacon, tomato and a slice of cheese (in that order)

7. Put the baking sheet with the assembled, open-faced sandwiches onto the top shelf of the oven and broil until cheese begins melt

8. Once the cheese has begun to melt, remove the baking sheet from the oven and immediately transfer the sandwiches from the baking sheet to plates and serve immediately

Spicy Maple Slow Cooker Chicken Sandwiches

8 servings

INGREDIENTS:

4 large chicken breasts, skinless, boneless

1 cup ketchup

2 tablespoons mustard

2 teaspoons lemon juice

¼ teaspoon garlic powder

½ cup maple syrup

2 tablespoons Worcestershire sauce

½ teaspoon chili powder

2 dashes hot pepper sauce (to taste)

1 small onion, chopped

8 sandwich rolls, split

INSTRUCTIONS:

1. Arrange the 8 chicken breasts on the bottom of the slow cooker

2. In a medium-sized mixing bowl, whisk together the ketchup, mustard, lemon juice, garlic powder, maple syrup, Worcestershire sauce, chili powder, and hot sauce until well blended

3. Stir in the onion

4. Pour the mixture over the chicken in the slow cooker

5. Set the cooker to Low, and cook for 6 hours

6. After cooking for 6 hours, use two forks to shred the chicken

7. After all the chicken has been shredded, cook on Low for an additional 30 minutes

8. After 30 minutes, pile the chicken on the sandwich rolls and serve

THE MAPLE SYRUP
COOKBOOK

SNACKS

Nutty Maple Popcorn

10 servings

INGREDIENTS:

Non-stick cooking spray (vegetable oil)

1 cup maple syrup

½ cup peanuts, shelled, roasted, salted

½ cup cashews, roasted, salted

9 cups popped popcorn, unflavored

INSTRUCTIONS:

1. Line 2 rimmed baking sheets with parchment paper

2. Spray the interior of a large mixing bowl with the cooking spray

3. Fill the oiled bowl with the popcorn and nuts

4. In a saucepan over medium heat, heat the maple syrup until it reaches 236°F on a candy thermometer

236°F, pour it over the popcorn and nuts

6. Quickly toss the popcorn/nuts/maple syrup mixture with a large spoon lightly coated with cooking oil spray

7. As soon as the hot maple syrup is distributed through the popcorn and peanuts, scoop about ¼ cup of the maple/popcorn/peanut mixture and place it on a prepared cookie sheet

8. Repeat step 7, working quickly, placing clumps of the maple/popcorn/peanut mixture about ½-inch apart

   NOTE: Shapes will be irregular; that's OK

9. Let the "clumps" cool to harden

10. Serve or store in a sealed container

254 Calorie Fruit & Maple Recovery Smoothie

2 servings

INGREDIENTS:

1 cup fresh or frozen strawberries

¾ cup fat-free Greek yogurt

½ frozen banana, cut in chunks

½ cup cold water

¼ cup quick-cooking oats

¼ cup maple syrup

4 ice cubes

pinch of nutmeg

INSTRUCTIONS:

1. Put the strawberries, yogurt, banana. water, oats, maple syrup, and ice cubes
 into a blender

2. Put the cap on the blender and blend the ingredients until they form a smooth, lump-free drink

3. Divide the liquid equally between 2 glasses and sprinkle ½ pinch of nutmeg on the top of the liquid in each glass

4. Serve immediately

Maple Chunky Beef Stew

6 servings

INGREDIENTS:

¼ cup all-purpose flour

Kosher salt and freshly ground black pepper (to taste)

1½ pounds beef, cut into half inch cubes

3 Tablespoons extra-virgin olive oil, divided

2 cloves garlic, chopped

1 large onion, sliced

1 stalk of celery, chopped

1 can (19 ounce) of tomatoes

½ cup dry red wine

½ cup maple syrup

4 medium size potatoes, cubed

2 large carrots, sliced

½ cup of water

INSTRUCTIONS:

1. Preheat oven to 325°F

2. Put flour, salt, pepper and beef into a gallon size a plastic bag; seal it and shake until the beef is coated

3. In a large skillet over medium heat, heat 1 Tablespoon of the oil and then add half of the coated beef and brown on all sides

4. When the beef has been browned, transfer it to a 3-quart casserole dish

5. Add another Tablespoon of oil to the skillet and brown the other half of the coated beef

6. When the beef has been browned, transfer it to the casserole dish with the first batch of browned beef

7. Add the last Tablespoon of oil to the skillet and add the garlic and onion and sauté until tender

4. When soft, transfer the sautéed garlic and onion to the casserole dish with the beef

5. Add the celery, tomatoes, wine, maple syrup, potatoes, carrots and water to the casserole (along with the beef, garlic and onion); give it a quick stir and cover

6. Put the covered casserole onto the center rack of the oven and bake at 325°F for four hours

7. Once cooked, ladle into bowls and serve

NOTE: this recipe works well in a slow cooker as well (set on low for 8 hours)

Orange-Maple Glazed Salmon

4 servings

INGREDIENTS:

> 4 single portion salmon fillets
>
> 4 tablespoons maple syrup
>
> 3 tablespoons apple cider vinegar
>
> 1½ oranges, juiced and zested

INSTRUCTIONS:

1. In a medium-sized glass bowl whisk together the orange zest, orange juice, maple syrup and vinegar

2. Place the salmon fillets into the bowl with the orange/maple/vinegar mixture, and spoon the mixture over the fillets

3. Cover the bowl and transfer to the to the refrigerator for 45 minutes

4. Preheat oven to 400°F

5. Lightly grease a 9-inch x 13-inch baking dish (I like to use glass for fish)

6. Place the marinated salmon fillets in the prepared baking dish

7. Put the baking dish with the salmon onto the center rack of the oven and bake for 20 minutes at 400°F

8. In a small saucepan over medium heat, add the salmon marinade in a sauce pan over medium and heat and whisk it until it reduces to a thick, almost jam-like, consistency

9. When the salmon has been properly cooked, immediately transfer the filets to plates, top with the reduced marinade and serve.

Maple-Thyme Marinated Hanger Steak

4 servings

INGREDIENTS:

2 pounds hanger steak

½ cup maple syrup

2 shallots, peeled and sliced

1 ounce fresh thyme

½ cup water

1 Tablespoon Kosher salt

1 teaspoon freshly ground black pepper

INSTRUCTIONS:

1. In a medium-sized mixing bowl, whisk together the maple syrup, shallots, thyme, water, salt, and pepper

2. Transfer the maple/shallot/spice mixture to a shallow dish

3. Place the steak in the dish with the maple/shallot/spice mixture and spoon the mixture over the steak

4. Cover the dish with the steak and marinade and put it in the fridge for 24 hours (turning at least once during that time)

5. After the steak has been marinated for 24 hours, preheat the grill

6. When the grill is hot, brush oil the grill and when the flames have died down, place the steak the grill

7. Brush the steak with the excess marinade (if there is a flare-up, move the steaks out of the flame)

8. Grill the steak for about 5 minutes on each side for medium rare

9. When it has been cooked to your liking, remove the steak from the grill and let it rest for 5 to 10 minutes before slicing and serving (serve immediately after slicing)

Maple and Mustard-Glazed Salmon

4 servings

INGREDIENTS:

2 tablespoons maple syrup

2 tablespoons whole-grain mustard

4 salmon fillets (about 1½ pounds total)

Kosher salt and freshly ground black pepper

Lemon wedges, for serving

INSTRUCTIONS:

1. Preheat the oven to 450°F

2. In a medium-sized mixing bowl, whisk together the maple syrup and mustard

3. Season both sides of the salmon fillets generously with the salt and pepper

4. Brush the seasoned salmon fillets with the maple/mustard mixture and set them aside

5. Set the oven to broil

6. Put the salmon fillets skin-side down on an oven-proof dish and give them another liberal brush of the maple/mustard mixture

7. Put the dish with the salmon on the top rack in the oven and broil until the maple/mustard mixture is well-caramelized and the fish is just cooked through (about 8 to 10 minutes, depending on the thickness of the fillet)

8. When the salmon is properly cooked, serve it immediately, garnished with the lemon wedges

Pan-seared Chicken Breasts with Soy Maple Glaze

4 servings

INGREDIENTS:

2 cups maple syrup

¼ cup soy sauce

1 cup water

¼ cup granulated maple sugar

1 piece (2 inches) fresh ginger, sliced

3 whole cloves garlic

4 stars star anise

2 Tablespoons whole coriander seeds

1 Tablespoon of extra-virgin olive oil

4 chicken breasts, boneless skinless

INSTRUCTIONS:

1. Put the maple syrup, soy sauce, water, maple sugar, ginger, garlic, star anise and coriander into a saucepan and simmer for 20 minutes

2. After 20 minutes, strain the simmered ingredients through fine mesh sieve into a bowl and set aside

3. Preheat oven to 325°F

4. In a large skillet over high heat, heat the olive oil and pan sear the chicken

5. Put the seared chicken into a shallow baking pan and pour the strained glaze over the top of the chicken

6. Transfer the baking dish with the chicken, uncovered, to the top rack in the oven and bake at 325°F for 15 minutes, basting every five minutes

7. Once fully cooked, let the chicken rest for 5 to 10 minutes before serving

Lemon/Maple Scallops

4 servings

INGREDIENTS:

1 tablespoon butter

1 shallot, minced

2 Tablespoons lemon juice

¼ cup dry white wine

1 teaspoon lemon zest, minced

¼ cup maple syrup

⅓ cup cream

½ tablespoon pink peppercorns, crushed

Kosher salt (to taste)

2 tablespoons of oil

1½ pounds of large scallops

INSTRUCTIONS:

1. In a medium skillet over medium heat, melt the butter

2. Add the shallot to the melted butter and sauté for 3 minutes

3. Add the lemon juice and wine to the sautéed shallot and simmer until it is reduced by half.

4. Stir the lemon zest and maple syrup in with the lemon juice, wine and shallot; bring the mixture to a boil

5. Add the cream to the skillet and simmer, stirring, for 3 minutes

6. Add the peppercorns to the cream/lemon/maple/wine/shallot mixture and season, to taste with salt

7. Set aside the skillet, keeping the peppercorn/cream/lemon/maple/wine/shallot mixture warm

8. In a large skillet over high heat, heat the oil

9. When the oil is hot, gently cook the scallops 1 minute on each side

10. After the 2 minutes of cooking, divide the scallops evenly on 4 plates and then pour ¼ of the sauce (peppercorn/cream/lemon/maple/wine/shallot) over each serving

11. Serve immediately

Maple Roast Chicken

6 servings

INGREDIENTS:

1 lemon, halved

1 whole chicken (about 3 ½ pounds)

Kosher salt and freshly ground black pepper, to taste

¼ cup extra-virgin olive oil, plus more for drizzling on the chicken

½ cup maple syrup

INSTRUCTIONS:

1. Preheat the oven to 400°F

2. Pat the chicken dry inside and out and place it in a roasting pan

3. Push the lemon into the cavity of the chicken

4. Tie the chicken's legs together with the kitchen string

5. Drizzle a little oil (about 1 Tablespoon) evenly over the chicken

6. Season the oiled chicken with the salt and pepper

7. Transfer the roasting pan with the chicken to the center rack of the oven and roast at 400°F for 30 minutes

8. In a small mixing bowl, whisk together the ¼ cup of oil with the maple syrup

9. After the chicken has cooked for 30 minutes, remove the pan from the oven and drizzle the entire chicken with the oil/maple syrup mixture

10. Reduce the oven temperature to 375°F, return the chicken to the oven, and roast for 25 minutes more.

11. After 25 minutes, baste the chicken with the pan drippings and then cook until the juices run clear or until an instant-read thermometer inserted in the thigh reads 165°F (about an additional 20 minutes)

12. When the chicken is fully cooked, remove the roasting pan from the oven and transfer the chicken to a cutting board.

      NOTE: the drippings remaining in the pan make the base for a nice gravy

13. Let the chicken rest for at least 10 minutes before carving and serving

Rosemary-Maple Pork Tenderloin

4 servings

INGREDIENTS:

1 pork tenderloin (about 1 pound)

¼ teaspoon Kosher salt

¼ teaspoon freshly ground black pepper

2 tablespoons extra-virgin olive oil

½ cup Marsala wine

8 ounce baby portabella mushrooms, sliced

1 medium shallot, finely chopped

2 cups beef broth (suggest: reduced sodium)

½ cup maple syrup

3 sprigs fresh rosemary

INSTRUCTIONS:

1. Season the pork with salt and pepper

2. Preheat large sauté pan skillet on medium-high for 3 minutes

3. Add the oil to the hot skillet

4. Add the tenderloin to the hot oil and cook for 5 minutes, turning occasionally, to brown all sides

5. Remove the pork from pan, set it aside (covered to retain warmth)

6. Remove the skillet from heat and pour in the Marsala

7. Put the skillet back on medium heat and stir in mushrooms and shallots

8. Stirring constantly, cook the wine/ mushroom/shallot mixture until the wine is reduces by half (about 3 minutes)

9. When the wine is reduced by about half, stir in broth, maple syrup, and whole rosemary sprigs

10. Cook the wine/mushroom/broth/maple mixture for 1 minute and then return tenderloin to the skillet; cover and cook 10–12 minutes (or until pork is 145°F), turning pork occasionally

11. When the pork is fully cooked, transfer it to a cutting board and let it rest 10 minutes before slicing

12. Continue to cook sauce until thickened (about 5 additional minutes)

13. Once the tenderloin has been rested, slice it into 1-inch-thick slices, top the slices with the sauce and serve

Slow Cooker Maple-Braised Pork Chops

10 servings

INGREDIENTS:

3 tablespoons all-purpose flour

Kosher salt and freshly ground pepper

10 pork loin chops (3 ounces each)

3 tablespoons extra-virgin olive oil

1 small yellow onion, finely chopped

1 clove garlic, minced

2 teaspoons chili powder

¾ cup chicken broth

¾ cup maple syrup

3 tablespoons apple cider vinegar

2 tablespoons Worcestershire sauce

2 tablespoons finely chopped fresh chives (for garnish)

INSTRUCTIONS:

1. In a shallow dish, sift together the flour, ¾ teaspoon salt, and ½ teaspoon pepper

2. Dredge the chops in the seasoned flour, covering all surfaces and shake off any excess

3. In a large skillet over medium-high heat, warm the oil

4. Two at a time, brow the chops (about 4 minutes each side)

5. When the chops have been browned arrange the evenly on the bottom of the stoneware insert of the slow cooker

6. Once all the chops have been browned, drain off all but a thin coating of fat in the skillet and return it to medium-high heat

7. Put the onion, garlic, and chili powder into the hot skillet and sauté until the onions start to become translucent

8. Pour in the broth into the skillet with the onion, garlic and chili powder and stir, scraping up the browned bits on the bottom of the pan with the spoon

9. Stir the maple syrup, vinegar, and Worcestershire sauce into the broth/onion/garlic mixture and bring to a boil

10. As soon as the contents of the skillet reach a boil, pour it all over the pork chops in the slow cooker

11. Put the cover on the slow cooker and cook until the chops are tender and the sauce is thick (4 hours on High or 8 hours on Low)

12. Once the chops are properly cooked, put them on plates, top with the sauce, garnish with the chives, and serve

THE MAPLE SYRUP
COOKBOOK

SIDE DISHES

Maple Roasted Asparagus

6 servings

INGREDIENTS:

1 bunch of asparagus (about 1 pound), washed, stem ends trimmed

2 cloves of garlic, thinly sliced

1 Tablespoon extra-virgin olive oil

1 Tablespoon maple syrup

1 Tablespoon Balsamic vinegar

1 Tablespoon fresh thyme leaves, coarsely chopped

Kosher salt and freshly ground black pepper (to taste)

INSTRUCTIONS:

1. Preheat oven to 450°F

2. Put the asparagus spears on a rimmed baking sheet

3. Add the garlic, oil, maple syrup, and vinegar to the asparagus and toss gently to coat evenly

4. Arrange the coated asparagus evenly over the surface of the baking sheet

5. Season the coated asparagus with the salt and pepper

6. Put the baking sheet with the asparagus onto the middle shelf of the oven and roast at 450°F for 7 minutes

7. After 7 minutes, turn the asparagus and then roast for an additional 7 minutes

8. Once the asparagus is cooked, remove it from the oven and transfer it to a serving dish

9. Sprinkle the asparagus in on the serving dish with the thyme and serve immediately

Maple Baked Beans

6 servings

INGREDIENTS:

2 cup dried Navy beans

6 strips bacon

1 onion chopped

1 teaspoon dried mustard (suggest Colman's)

1 teaspoon Kosher salt

½ cup maple syrup

I pork hock (fresh or smoked, I prefer smoked)

2 tablespoons butter

2 tablespoons brown sugar

INSTRUCTIONS:

1. Preheat oven to 325°F

2. In a large pot over high heat, bring 6 cups of water to a boil, add the Navy beans, reduce the heat and simmer the navy beans until they are tender (about 20 minutes)

3. When the Navy beans are cooked, drain them and reserve cooking liquid

5. Transfer the cooked Navy beans to a large mixing bowl

4. Line the pot in which you cooked the beans with the bacon

5. Toss the onions together with the cooked beans in the large mixing bowl

6. In a different large mixing bowl, combine 2 cups of bean cooking liquid, the mustard, salt and maple syrup; stir until well mixed

7. Place half the bean/onion mixture on bacon strips in pot

8. Place the pork hock on the beans and then put the rest of the bean/onion mixture on top of the hock

9. Carefully pour the cooking liquid/syrup mixture over the beans and put the lid on the pot

10. Transfer the full pot to the bottom shelf of the oven and cook at 325°F until the pork hock is fully cooked and pulling away from the bone (about 3 hours)

NOTE: Check the pot periodically, if the beans begin to look dry, add more cooking liquid.

11. Once the pork hock is cooked, remove the pot from the oven and take off the lid

12. In a small mixing bowl, mash butter and brown sugar into a paste

13. Scatter butter/sugar paste over beans and place the pot back in the oven, uncovered, for an additional 30 minutes

14. After 30 minutes, take the pot of baked beans from the oven and serve

Quick Maple Corn Bread with Maple Butter

9 Servings

INGREDIENTS:

1 cup all-purpose flour

1 cup cornmeal

1½ teaspoons baking powder

½ teaspoon Kosher salt

1 cup non-fat milk

¼ cup canola oil

1½ Tablespoons maple syrup

1 egg, lightly beaten

Maple Butter:

½ cup softened unsalted butter

¼ cup maple syrup

INSTRUCTIONS:

1. Preheat oven to 400°F

2. Grease a 9-inch square baking pan

3. In a large mixing bowl, sift together the flour, cornmeal, baking powder and salt

4. In a separate medium-sized mixing bowl, whisk together the milk, oil, maple syrup and egg

5. Pour the milk/maple/egg mixture over the flour/cornmeal mixture and stir until just combined and moist (do not over mix)

6. Spread the batter evenly in the prepared baking pan, put the pan on the middle rack of the oven and bake at 400°F until a toothpick inserted in the center comes out clean (20-25 minutes)

7. When the cornbread is finished baking remove it from the oven and serve immediately with maple butter

Maple Butter Instructions:

1. Put the butter and maple syrup into the bowl of an electric mixer and beat on medium until thoroughly combined

NOTE: this maple butter will last 5 weeks if stored in an airtight container and refrigerated

Maple Praline Pecans

8 servings

INGREDIENTS:

1 Tablespoon egg whites, stirred

2 cups pecans

½ cup granulated maple sugar

½ teaspoon cinnamon

½ teaspoon nutmeg

INSTRUCTIONS:

1. Preheat oven to 300°F

2. Line 2 rimmed baking sheets with parchment paper

3. Put the pecans in a large mixing bowl

4. In separate small mixing bowl, combine the maple sugar with the cinnamon and nutmeg

5. Pour the egg whites over the nuts and stir until the nuts are moistened on all sides

6. Pour the sugar/spice mixture over the pecans nuts and stir to coat thoroughly

7. Spread the coated nuts on the prepared baking sheets and put the baking sheets with the nuts into the oven and bake at 300°F for 15 minutes

8. Once the pecans have baked for 15 minutes, turn them all over and bake for an additional 15 minutes

9. After the nuts have had a total 30 minutes baking, remove them from the oven and allow them to cool completely

10. Once cool, break then apart and serve or store in an airtight container

Old Fashioned Maple Fudge

18 servings

INGREDIENTS:

2 cups maple syrup

⅓ cup cream

INSTRUCTIONS:

1. Grease a loaf pan with butter (suggest glass)

2. In a sauce pan over medium heat, whisk together the maple syrup and cream and then cook it until it reaches the soft boil stage

3. As soon as it reaches the soft boil stage, take it off the heat and let it cool to 150 degrees

4. Pour the maple/cream mixture into a medium mixing bowl and whisk until thickened (this will take longer than you expect ... your arm will be tired)

5. Scrape the thickened mixture into buttered loaf pan, smooth the top, and put in the fridge to cool

6. Once cool, cut and serve

NOTE: a fun variation is to dip the maple fudge in melted chocolate and then dust with maple sugar; allow to cool and set up before serving

Mom's Maple Chewies (Cookies)

24 servings

INGREDIENTS:

2 cups all-purpose flour

½ teaspoon baking soda

½ teaspoon ground ginger

¼ teaspoon cinnamon

½ teaspoon Kosher salt

1 stick unsalted butter, at room temperature

1 cup dark brown sugar

1 teaspoon vanilla extract

1 egg

¾ cup maple syrup

INSTRUCTIONS:

1. In a medium-sized mixing bowl, sift together the flour, baking soda, ginger, cinnamon, and salt

2. In a large mixing bowl, beat together the butter and sugar until light and fluffy (about 4 minutes)

3. Add the vanilla and egg to the butter/sugar mixture and beat until well combined

4. Add the maple syrup to the vanilla/egg/butter/sugar mixture and beat until well combined

5. Add half the flour/spice mixture to the maple/vanilla/egg/butter/sugar mixture and stir until it is until just incorporated

6. Add the remaining half of the flour and, again, stir until just incorporated

7. Use plastic wrap to cover bowl and put it in the fridge for 1 hour

8. Preheat the oven to 350°F

9. Line two rimmed baking sheets with parchment paper

10. Remove the dough from the fridge and place it, one tablespoon at a time, on the prepared baking sheets

NOTE: Keep the cookies three inches apart on the baking sheets

11. Put the baking sheets with the cookie dough into the oven and bake at 350°F until the cookies turn golden around the edges (about 10 minutes)

12. Once properly cooked, remove the baking sheets from the oven and let the cookies cool for 10 minutes on the sheets until transferring them to a cooling rack

13. Serve warm or wait for them to be fully cooled

Maple Shortbread

36 servings

INGREDIENTS:

Maple butter:

⅔ cup maple syrup

1 cup butter, at room temperature

Shortbread:

¾ cup maple butter

2 cups all-purpose flour

1 pinch Kosher salt

INSTRUCTIONS:

Maple butter:

1. In a small saucepan, bring the maple syrup to a boil and reduce it by half (about 15 minutes)

2. Once the maple syrup is reduced, remove it from heat and let it stand and reach room temperature

3. When the reduced maple syrup is cool, whisk in the butter until well blended and then put in the fridge until firm

Shortbread:

1. Put the maple butter, flour and salt in the bowl of a food processor and pulse until well combined

7. Take the maple/flour/salt out of the food processor and shape it into a ball and then flatten it into a disc shape

8. Wrap the processed maple/flour disc in plastic wrap and put it on a flat surface in the fridge until well chilled.

9. Preheat oven to 350°F

10. Retrieve the dough disc from the fridge and roll it out to a thickness of about ¼ inch

11. Cut the dough into wedges

>   NOTE: you can also use a cookie cutter to have your shortbread in specific shapes ... in this case, a maple leaf shaped cookie cutter might be appropriate

12. Place wedges about 2-inches apart on an ungreased cookie sheet and bake at 350°F until they are slightly golden brown (about 10-15 min)

13. When the shortbread wedges are fully cooked, remove them from the oven and allow them to cool on the sheet for 5 minutes before moving them to a cooling rack

14. Allow to fully cool prior to serving

Maple Brittle

12 servings

INGREDIENTS:

2 cups maple syrup

2 tablespoons butter

¼ teaspoons cream of tartar

few grains of Kosher salt

½ cup walnuts

INSTRUCTIONS:

1. Lightly grease a rimmed baking sheet

2. Spread the walnuts evenly on the prepared baking sheet

3. Combine the maple syrup, butter, cream of tartar and salt in a sauce pan

4. Over medium-high heat, boil the ingredients until syrup forms a very hard thread in cold water (280°F)

   NOTE: Don't stir the syrup or sugar crystals will form

3. Once the ingredient have reached temperature, pour the contents evenly over the walnuts on the baking sheet

3. When cooled completely, break the brittle into pieces and serve

Maple Cheesecake

8 servings

INGREDIENTS:

2 cups honey-style graham cracker crumbs

4 tablespoons butter, melted

¼ cup maple sugar

4 eggs, beaten

1 cup maple syrup

24 ounces cream cheese, softened

INSTRUCTIONS:

1. Preheat oven to 350°F

2. Lightly grease a 9-inch springform pan

3. In a medium-sized mixing bowl, combine the cracker crumbs, butter and maple sugar

4. When thoroughly combined, press the cracker crumb/butter/maple mixture into the bottom of the prepared spring pan

5. In a large mixing bowl combine the eggs, maple syrup, and cream cheese and beat until very smooth

6. Pour the egg/maple/cream cheese mixture over the crust

7. Put the filled spring pan on the middle rack of the oven and bake at 350°F for 1 hour

8. When the cheesecake is thoroughly cooked, remove it from the oven and allow it to cool completely in the pan

9. When the cheesecake has totally cooled down, remove it from the spring pan and transfer it to a serving platter

10. Refrigerate for 1 hour before slicing and serving

Maple Pots de Crème

4 servings

INGREDIENTS:

½ cup maple syrup

1½ cups heavy whipping cream

¼ teaspoon Kosher salt

4 egg yolks

½ teaspoon vanilla

Whipped cream for garnish

INSTRUCTIONS:

1. Preheat the oven to 300°F

2. In a sauce pan over medium heat, bring the maple syrup, cream and salt to a simmer

3. In a large mixing bowl, beat egg yolks with a whisk

4. Whisking the yolks, slowly add to them the maple/cream mixture to the eggs

5. When the yolks and maple/cream mixture are thoroughly combined, strain the mixture through a fine mesh sieve into a clean bowl (I use a large glass measuring cup with a spout)

6. Once through the sieve, pour the custard in the ramekins and put them in the bottom of a large roasting pan

7. Put the roasting pan on the middle shelf of the oven and fill the baking pan with hot water until it comes halfway up the sides of the ramekins

8. Bake until custards are set on top but slightly loose in the middle (about 50 minutes)

9. Once the custards are properly cooked, remove them from the water bath and set them aside to cool

10. When cooled, move them to the refrigerator for at least 2 hours before serving

11. After 2 hours (or more) in the fridge, serve with a dollop of whipped cream in each ramekin

Maple Walnut Snowballs

36 servings

INGREDIENTS:

1 cup unsalted butter, softened

½ cup confectioner's sugar, plus more for decoration

1 teaspoon vanilla extract

3 tablespoons maple syrup

¼ teaspoon Kosher salt

1½ cups medium to fine ground walnuts

2¼ cups all-purpose flour

INSTRUCTIONS:

1. In a large mixing bowl, cream the butter until it is light and fluffy

2. Add the confectioner's sugar vanilla to the creamed butter and cream for 1 minute

3. Add the vanilla, maple syrup and salt to the butter/sugar mixture and stir until blended

4. Add the walnuts to the vanilla/maple/butter/sugar mixture and stir until evenly distributed

5. While mixing, add the flour ¾ cup at a time to the nut/maple/butter/sugar mixture until thoroughly mixed, periodically scraping the sides of the bowl with a spatula to make sure all ingredients get thoroughly blended

6. Once all ingredients have been incorporated, scrape the dough together, wrap it in plastic, and put it in the fridge for 2 hours

7. Preheat the oven to 325°F

8. Line two rimmed baking sheets with a parchment paper

9. Remove the wrapped dough from the fridge, roll teaspoon-sized pieces of the chilled dough into 1-inch balls and put them on the baking sheets 1½ inches apart

10. Once filled with dough balls, put the baking sheets into the fridge for 5 minutes to re-chill the dough

11. After 5 minutes, take the baking sheets with the dough balls out of the fridge, put them in the oven, and bake t 325°F until the tops are just firm and the bottoms golden brown (about 20 minutes)

12. Once the dough balls have been properly cooked, take the trays out of the oven and set them on a rack to cool for 3 minutes

12. Put confectioner's sugar in a small bowl and one-by-one roll the warm cookie balls in the sugar, coating them well

13. Once a cookie ball has been rolled in the sugar, transfer it to a wire rack to cool; repeat until all the cookie balls have been rolled in sugar and placed on the rack

14. When the cookie balls are cook, either reroll them or liberally dust them with more confectioners' sugar

14. Serve or store in an airtight container at room temperature (for 2 to 3 days)

Maple Ice Cream

8 servings

INGREDIENTS:

⅔ cup maple syrup

1¾ cups heavy cream

¾ cup whole milk

4 large egg yolks

¼ teaspoon fine salt

INSTRUCTIONS:

1. Fill a large bowl half way with ice and water (to make an ice bath)

2. In a small sauce pan over medium heat, heat the maple syrup to a simmer and continue to simmer until it's reduced by a quarter (about 5 minutes) and then take the sauce pan off the heat and set it aside

3. In a medium saucepan over medium heat, combine the cream and milk and heat until just simmering (about 5 minutes)

4. In a medium oven proof bowl, whisk the yolks until they get lighter in color and start to thicken (about 2 minutes)

5. Once the cream/milk mixture is simmering, remove the sauce pan from heat and pour about ½ cup into the yolks, while whisking constantly

6. Return the sauce pan with the remaining cream/milk mixture to medium and whisk in the cream/milk/yolk mixture

7. Reduce the heat to medium low and cook the cream/milk/yolk mixture, stirring constantly, until it thickens and coats the back of a spoon (about 3 minutes)

> NOTE: You are making a custard. One way to test to see if it is thick enough is to make a line in it by running your finger through it; the line should hold and not run back into itself.

8. When at the proper consistency, remove the custard from heat and stir in the maple syrup reduction and the salt until thoroughly combined

9. Pour the mapled and salted custard through a fine-mesh strainer into a large heatproof bowl and place it into the ice bath (don't let any water run into the custard) until the custard is chilled (about 40 minutes)

10. After the temperature has been brought down in the water bath, cover the bowl and put it in the fridge overnight

11. Once the ice cream base has been chilled, turn it into ice cream in an ice cream maker and following the manufacturer's instructions

Cranberry Apple Maple Pecan Loaf

1 loaf/12 servings

INGREDIENTS:

⅓ cup fresh orange juice

zest of one orange, finely grated

½ cup buttermilk plus 2 teaspoons

3 Tablespoons unsalted butter, melted

¼ cup unsweetened applesauce

1 large egg, slightly beaten

2 cups all-purpose flour

½ cup maple syrup

1 teaspoon Kosher salt

1 teaspoon baking powder

¼ teaspoon baking soda

1½ cups cranberries, coarsely chopped

¾ cup pecans, coarsely chopped

INSTRUCTIONS:

1. Preheat oven to 375°F

2. Grease a 9-inch x 5-inch loaf pan

3. In a medium glass mixing bowl, whisk together the orange juice, zest, buttermilk, butter, applesauce and egg

4. In a large mixing bowl, sift together the flour, sugar, salt, baking powder and baking soda

5. Stir the orange/butter/applesauce/egg mixture into the flour/sugar/sale mixture until the dry ingredients are just wet

6. Add cranberries and pecans into the combined mixture and stir until they are evenly distributed (do not over mix)

7. Pour mixture into the prepared loaf pan

8. Transfer the batter-filled loaf pan to the middle rack of the oven and bake at 375°F for 20 minutes

9. After baking for 20 minutes, reduce heat to 350°F and cook until the top is golden brown and a knife inserted in center comes out clean (an additional 35-45 minutes)

10. When the bread is thoroughly cooked, transfer it to a cooling rack and allow it to cool in the pan for 10 minutes

11. After it has cooled for 10 minutes, turn the loaf out onto the cooling rack and allow it to cool completely before slicing and serving

Maple Pumpkin Spice Bread

1 loaf/12 servings

INGREDIENTS:

1 cup whole-wheat flour

1 cup all-purpose flour

1 Tablespoon ground cinnamon

2 teaspoons ground ginger

1½ teaspoon baking powder

½ teaspoon baking soda

½ teaspoon ground nutmeg

½ teaspoon ground allspice

1 cup maple syrup

½ cup grape canola oil

2 large eggs

1 cup pumpkin purée

1 teaspoon vanilla extract

½ cup chopped pecans

INSTRUCTIONS:

1. Preheat oven to 350°F

2. Grease and flour a 9-inch x 5-inch loaf pan

3. In a large mixing bowl, whisk together the flours, cinnamon, ginger, baking powder, baking soda, nutmeg, and allspice

4. In a separate large mixing bowl, whisk together the maple syrup and oil

5. Whisk into the maple/oil mixture the eggs and then whisk in the pumpkin and vanilla

6. Stir the flour/spice mixture into maple/pumpkin mixture until thoroughly combined

7. Add the pecans to the flour/spice/maple/pumpkin mixture and stir until they are evenly distributed

8. Scrape the dough (pecan/ flour/spice/maple/pumpkin mixture) into the prepared loaf pan

9. Put the dough-filled loaf pan onto the middle rack of the oven and bake at 350°F until toothpick inserted in center of loaf comes out clean (40 to 50 minutes)

10. When the bread is properly cooked, transfer it from the oven to a cooling rack and allow it to cool in the pan for 5 minutes

11. After cooling in the pan for 5 minutes, turn the cake out of the pan onto the cooling rack to cool down further

12. Serve warm

Maple Bacon Bread

1 loaf/12 servings

INGREDIENTS:

1¼ cups lukewarm water

2¼ teaspoons instant yeast

2 tablespoons maple syrup

3¼ cups bread flour

¼ teaspoon Kosher salt

½ pound bacon, cooked until crisp, crumbled

2 tablespoons bacon fat

INSTRUCTIONS:

1. In a large skillet over medium high heat, cook the bacon until it is extra crispy

2. Set the bacon on paper towels to drain and reserve 2 tablespoons of the fat from the pan to use later in this recipe

3. In the mixing bowl of a stand mixer with a bread hook, combine the water, yeast, maple syrup, and bread flour and knead until the dough becomes smooth and elastic

4. Add the salt, crumbled bacon, and bacon fat to the dough and continue kneading until all the ingredients are well integrated

5. When the dough has been fully kneaded, cover the bowl with the dough with a clean kitchen towel plastic wrap and set aside until the dough has doubled in size (about 1 hour)

6. Preheat the oven to 350°F

7. Line a rimmed baking sheet with parchment paper

8. Once the dough has doubled in size, turn it out onto a floured work surface and press it gently to release some of the collected air

9. Form the dough into a tight ball, sealing the seam at the bottom

10. Place the dough, seam-side down, on the prepared baking sheet

11. Cover the dough with a clean kitchen towel and plastic set aside until it has doubled in size (about 40 minutes)

12. Remove the towel, put the baking sheet with the dough onto the center rack of the oven and bake at 350°F until it is nicely browned (about 35 minutes)

13. When the bread is fully cooked, remove it from the oven and set it on a cooling rack to cool completely before slicing and serving

Maple Oatmeal Bread

2 loaves/24 servings

INGREDIENTS:

2½ cups boiling water

1 cup rolled oats

1 package dry yeast

¾ cup maple syrup

2 teaspoons Kosher salt

1 tablespoon oil

5 cups all-purpose flour

INSTRUCTIONS:

1. Put the oats into a large mixing bowl, pour the boiling water over the oats and then set it aside for an hour.

2. After the oats have soaked for an hour, stir into them the yeast, maple syrup, salt, and oil

3. Thoroughly mix 3 cups of the flour into the oats/yeast/maple mixture

4. With a clean kitchen towel, cover the bowl containing the flour/ the oats/yeast/maple mixture and set it aside for an hour to rise

5. After it has risen for an hour add more flour, half a cup at a time, until the dough is the correct consistency for bread (not too wet or sticky)

6. Knead the dough for 10 minutes

7. Grease two 5-inch x 9-inch loaf pans

8. Cut the dough into two equal pieces, shape each half into a loaf and place a loaf in each of the prepared loaf pans

9. With a clean kitchen towel, cover the dough-filled loaf pans and set them aside for another 45 minutes to rise

10. Preheat the oven to bake at 350°F

11. Put the dough-filled loaf pans on the center rack of the oven and bake at 350°F until the tops are well browned (about 45 minutes)

12. When the bread is finished cooking, remove the loaves from the pans and set them on a cooling rack

13. Allow the bread to cool completely before slicing

Maple Banana Bread

1 loaf/12 servings

INGREDIENTS:

½ cup butter, melted

½ cup maple syrup

1 egg

2 ripe bananas (the riper the better)

½ teaspoon maple extract

3 tablespoons milk

2 cups all-purpose flour

1 teaspoon baking soda

½ teaspoon baking powder

¼ cup chopped walnuts

3 tablespoons granulated white sugar

INSTRUCTIONS:

1. Preheat the oven to 350°F

2. Grease a 5-inch x 9-inch loaf pan

3. In a large mixing bowl, combine the butter and maple syrup

4. Beat in the egg and bananas into the butter/maple mixture, leaving a few small banana chunks

5. Stir the maple extract and milk into the egg/banana/butter/maple mixture

6. In a separate large mixing bowl, sift together the flour, baking soda, and baking powder

7. Stir the banana/maple/mild mixture into the flour mixture just until the flour mixture is moistened

8. In a small mixing bowl combine the nuts and sugar

9. Transfer the flour/banana/maple mixture into the prepared loaf pan

10. Sprinkle the nut/sugar mixture evenly over the batter in the loaf pan

11.Place the dough-filled loaf pan onto the middle rack of the oven and bake at 350°F until a knife inserted in the center of the loaf comes out clean (about 50 minutes)

12. When the bread is properly cooked, let it cool in the pan, on a wire rack, for 5 minutes

13. After 5 minutes of cooling in the pan, turn the loaf out onto the rack to let cool completely

Gluten Free Maple Walnut Bread

1 loaf/12 servings

INGREDIENTS:

2¼ cups gluten free flour blend (suggest: King Arthur)

⅔ cup tapioca flour

⅔ cup potato starch

1 tablespoon baking powder

½ teaspoon baking soda

1½ teaspoons xanthan gum

1½ teaspoons ground cinnamon

1 teaspoon Kosher salt

1 stick unsalted butter, softened

1 cup maple syrup

1 cup buttermilk, at room temperature

2 large eggs

¾ cup chopped walnuts

INSTRUCTIONS:

1. Heat oven to 350°F

2. Grease a 9inch x 5-inch loaf pan

3. In a large mixing bowl, sift together the flours, starch, baking powder, baking soda, xanthan gum, cinnamon and salt

4. In a small sauce pan over medium heat, cook the butter, stirring occasionally, until butter turns a nut brown color and then remove the pan from the heat and set it aside

5. In a different large mixing bowl whisk together the maple syrup, buttermilk and eggs and then stir in browned butter

6. Add the maple/milk/egg mixture to the flour/starch/spice mixture and stir until just combined

7. Add the walnuts into the maple/milk/egg/flour/starch/spice mixture and stir until the nuts are evenly distributed

8. Pour the mixture into the prepared loaf pan

9. Put the dough-filled loaf pan onto the middle shelf of the oven and bake at 350°F until the bread has risen and a toothpick stuck in the middle of the loaf comes out clean (55 to 60 minutes)

10. When the bread is fully cooked, remove it from the oven and allow it to cool in the pan for 10 minutes before out turning onto a cooling rack

11. Allow the bread to cool fully before slicing and serving

THE MAPLE SYRUP
COOKBOOK

COCKTAILS

The Maple Leaf

1 serving

INGREDIENTS:

>   1½ ounces bourbon whiskey
>
>   ½ ounce maple syrup
>
>   ½ ounce fresh lemon juice

INSTRUCTIONS:

1. Pour all the ingredients into a cocktail shaker filled with ice

2. Shake until well mixed (about 15 seconds)

3. Strain into a cocktail glass

Bourbon Maple Cider

4 servings

INGREDIENTS:

4 ounces bourbon whiskey

4 ounces applejack

2 ounces maple syrup

1 dash Angostura bitters

16 ounces hard cider

INSTRUCTIONS:

1. Pour the bourbon, apple jack, maple syrup, and bitters into a cocktail shaker filled with ice

2. Shake until well mixed (about 15 seconds)

3. Strain, distributing evenly, into 4 ice-filled cocktail glasses

4. Top each glass with 4 ounces of cider

The Maple Old Fashioned

1 serving

INGREDIENTS:

2 ounces bourbon whiskey

½ ounces maple syrup

Slice of orange

Dash of bitters

INSTRUCTIONS:

1. Pour the maple syrup into a glass

2. Add 3 or 4 ice cubes to the maple syrup and pour in bourbon a bit at a time, stirring in between so it properly combines with the syrup

3. Add a splash of bitters (about ¼ ounce)

4. Rub an orange slice around the inside of a rocks glass and add fresh ice

5. Strain the bourbon mixture into the rocks glass

6. Garnish with the orange slice

BONUS RECIPE

This recipe comes from my second volume of maple syrup recipes *The Maple Syrup Cookbook Volume 2 - 40 More Easy, Delicious, & Healthy Maple Syrup Recipes for Breakfast Lunch & Dinner*. This is always a big hit in our household, sometimes plain and sometimes "a la mode" with vanilla ice cream.

Maple Almond Squares

12 servings

INGREDIENTS:

Crust

1¼ cups all-purpose flour

⅓ cup light brown sugar

½ cup butter, softened

Topping

1 cup maple syrup

½ cup light brown sugar

2 large eggs, beaten well

2 tablespoons butter, melted

1 ½ teaspoons vanilla

2 tablespoons all-purpose flour

¼ teaspoon Kosher salt

1 cup chopped almonds, divided

INSTRUCTIONS:

1. Preheat the oven to 375°F

2. Greased an 8-inch square baking dish

3. In a medium-sized mixing bowl, sift together flour and sugar

4. Cut the butter into the flour/sugar mix and blend until the mixture resembles coarse meal

5. Press the butter/flour/sugar mixture into the bottom of the prepared baking dish

6. Put the filled baking dish onto the middle rack of the oven and bake at 375°F for 15 minutes

7. After baking for 15 minutes, remove the baking dish with the crust from the oven and allow it to cool

8. Reduce the oven temperature to 350°F

8. In a medium-sized mixing bowl, whisk together the maple syrup and sugar

9. Whisk the eggs into the maple/sugar mixture

10. Stir the butter, vanilla, flour, salt and ¾ cup of the almonds, mixing well until thoroughly mixed

11. Pour the maple/sugar/egg/butter/vanilla/four mixture evenly onto the crust in the baking dish

12. Sprinkle the remaining ¼ cup of almonds on top of the ingredients in the baking dish

13. Return the baking dish to the oven and bake at 350°F until slightly browned and bubbly (25-30 minutes)

14. Once finished cooking, remove the baking dish from the oven and set it on a cooling rack to cool completely in the baking dish

15. Once completely cooled, refrigerate for a minimum of 2 hours

15. Once chilled, cut into squares and serve

About the Author

Jean LeGrand is unsure whether he cooks because he likes to eat or that he eats because he likes to cook.

"Actually," he says, "I cook for a number of reasons beyond just paying the bills." Here are some of the reasons he offers:

"I think cooking is an art, a form of self-expression, so I cook to create something new."

"I like how cooking brings family and friends together."

"I enjoy the creative process and get a kick out of watching my friends and family enjoy my creations."

"The exploration aspect of cooking -- new tastes and new techniques -- is very exciting."

"I'm good at it, so I get a great feeling of satisfaction and pride when I make a dish that brings compliments ... the biggest one being when things start to get quiet because everybody is enjoying the food experience so much that they forget to talk."

LeGrand writes recipe books because "I like the fact that I can take all the enjoyment I get from cooking and extend it beyond my circle of family and friends. It makes me happy that I'm helping people enjoy both the cooking and eating sides of great food."

Recipe Books by Best Selling Author Jean LeGrand include:

The Maple Syrup Cookbook Volume 2 - *Romantic Treats* - *Top Paleo Diet Recipes* - *Fruit Infused Water Recipes* - *FrankenFood Recipes #1* - *FrankenFood Recipes #2* - *Delicious & Healthy Paleo Recipes* - *Easter Brunch* - *Easter Dinner* - *Mother's Day Recipes* - *Irish Treats* - *Irish Dinner* - *Irish Drinks*

Can I Ask a Favor?

Thank you so much for reading my book. I hope you really liked it.

As you probably know, many people look at the reviews on Amazon before they decide to purchase a book.

If you liked the book, **could you please take a minute** to leave a review with your feedback?

Just go to Amazon.com, look up *Maple Cookbook - LeGrand,* go to the book's page) and scroll down until you see the orange "Write a customer review button", click it and write a few words about why you like the book.

A couple of minutes is all I'm asking for, and it would mean the world to me.

Thank you so much,

Jean

Printed in Great Britain
by Amazon.co.uk, Ltd.,
Marston Gate.

DEEPENING SERIES: Volume One

THRESHOLDS

Retreat-in-Daily Life

by
Dr. Catherine Al-Meten

Whales & Nightingales Press
Astoria, Oregon

To my family and friends in gratitude.

Library of Congress Cataloguing in Publication Date

Almeten, Catherine

    Thresholds: A Retreat-in-Daily Life

    1. Spirituality, 2. Psychology and Religion, 3. Inspiration. 4. Spiritual Life.

ISBN-13: 978-1495216244 (CreateSpace-Assigned)
ISBN-10: 1495216241

Week One
Day One. Joy Renewed, Joy in Compassion

"When you do things from your soul, you feel a river moving in you, a joy." -- Rumi

A Retreat-in-Daily Life guides you to discover and reawaken a sense of joy and compassion. Within the context of the life you are living, use this guide as a way to spend some time each day in quiet contemplation, prayer, meditation, and reflection. However you choose to enter into this experience, do so open to the movement of grace in your life. Listen for the 'still small voice' within that calls you to acts of compassion. Watch for signs and affirmations of the Presence of the Divine--ever present in your life.

Entering into sacred time and space is a matter of turning our attention towards the sacred and Divine. Each person discovers the holy in differently. Spirituality is not stagnant, but changes as we change. Be content with where you are at this time in your life. Regardless of what is going on in life or what age a person is, the sacred is present in some way.

Designed to be done over 40 days, it may also be done more slowly, over a longer period of time. Use this guide in a way that works for you, working your way through the exercises and meditations at your own pace.

A retreat-in-daily life occurs at the same time that both seasonal and religious holidays take place. Use the guide to enhance those experiences for yourself. Consider that every day is part of the Holy. Deepen your awareness each day of how you are connected to the sacred through all your experiences.

All the world's great religious and spiritual traditions honor the idea of setting aside each day to connect to the Divine. We are always in the process of rediscovering how the Divine informs and guides us in our daily life.

Rites and rituals like the Eucharist bring the past into the present moment, and allow us to be present in the most sacred moments. This 40-day retreat-in-daily life is a time to intentionally turn towards the Divine, God, Allah, the Creator, the Source--whatever word you choose to use to talk about the Sacred in your life. It is a time to renew your relationship, to reawaken the joy of that connection in your heart and your daily life.

As you begin this retreat, reflect on your life and the gifts, challenges, opportunities, burdens, and desires that are unique to you. Begin by spending a little time in reflection on how you are entering this experience. What hopes and fears do you have? What desires or challenges fill your mind and heart? What needs do you have that need to be healed?

Just for today, notice where joy is present in your life. Notice where joy is missing. What brings you peace? What blocks you from peace?

Be open to receiving the inspiration, consolation, and affirmation you needs as experience this daily life retreat.

How to do a daily life retreat.

Be simple. Set aside some time and a space where you will not be disturbed. You may set aside 5 minutes or a half hour. You may set up a quiet corner in your home or office, or you may go for a long walk. However you choose to do your retreat, focus on letting yourself be mindful and open to receiving what you need so that you can then share your blessings with others.

Pick the reflection questions that speak to your heart and experiences as well.

Allow yourself time and space to be still and quiet:

"There is so much noise in the world! May we learn to be silent in our hearts and before God." Pope Francis, 11/27/14

Let go, listen, watch, and feel the Presence of the Divine.

Choose one or two of the inspirational quotes or scriptures to inspire you. Take what speaks to you, and leave what does not. This is your retreat. Find ways to make this work into the life you are living

Inspirational Quotes.

From the Song of Solomon/Canticle of Canticles
"Many waters cannot quench love, neither can the floods drown it."

Romans 8:28 "And we know that God causes everything to work together for the good of those who love God and are called according to God's purpose for them."

Edward Abbey, "A great thirst is a great joy when quenched in time."

Mother Teresa, "God gives us things to share. God doesn't give us things to hold."

Reflections:

How am I preparing my heart for the holidays?

How am I experiencing joy in my life?

What is blocking my joy?

Where is my energy trapped in sorrow, fear, sadness, or anger?

What do I seek to discover or experience during this retreat-in-daily life?

Suggestions.

Use the quotations or thoughts for reflection.
Keep a journal or diary of your thoughts, reflections
Draw, paint, or sculpt as part of your meditation and prayer practice
Send someone you love a letter or postcard.
Give someone a small gift, something that holds meaning to you that you want to share. It could be an object, or some help (a recipe for a special dish or assistance doing the dishes), some information (point out a constellation in the night sky), or a book or poem.
Use this experience in whatever way helps you and fits your needs. Use this guide to deepen your connection with the Divine gifts within you and your life, and to awaken joy in your daily life.

Notes:

Day 2/40 Hope

"Beauty is the illumination of your soul."
John O'Donohue, Anam Cara

The concepts of Light and Hope come to mind when considering our spirituality. When setting out on a journey, we have no idea what awaits us. We have many expectations, and plans we hopes we will find what we are seeking. Yet we know, from experience, life never seems to go exactly according to plans. The unexpected, the change of direction, the obstacles on the pathway or the new doors that appear in the side of a stone wall we thought was forever closed, opens. As you take this journey, allow yourself to become more comfortable with what arises and unfolds. Let your expectations and plans fall away to what arrives instead.

For today, slow your pace a bit. Quiet your mind, and listen, and watch. Allow yourself to notice surprising messages, enlightening ideas, unexpected affirmations, and consolation. Be receptive to streams of Hope where you struggle or falter. Be open to tiny rays of Light that open your heart and mind to the answers and comfort you need. Let your Light radiate out from the center of your being to warm a friend, comfort one in mourning, and touch with the healing balm of Love, those in need.

Words of Inspiration.

Emily Dickinson (1830-1886)

Hope is the thing with feathers
That perches in the soul.
And sings the tune
Without the words
And never stops at all.

Oliver Goldsmith (1730-1774)

Hope, like the gleaming taper's light,
Adorns and cheers our way;
And still, as darker grows the night,
Emits a brighter ray.

John Muir. "How glorious a greeting the sun gives the mountains!"

Victor Frankel, "What is to give light is to endure burning."

N.P. Willis, "There they stand, the innumerable stars, shining in order like a living hymn written in light."

What inspires you and gives you Hope? What Lights your way?

Suggestions for today's reflection:

Go through the storehouse of your faith and spiritual bounty, and find the most precious of your gifts. Wrap yourself up in your finest garments of Hope, Light, and Love, and prepare yourself for the celebration of life that is yours each day. Discover , something of value, hidden away for too long, something that needs to be brought out, polished, and placed in a special spot of your home.

Create a special place in your home to represent your journey and your celebration of the Light that shines within you.

Stay up late tonight, or get up early tomorrow morning, and gaze into the night sky. Find something that points you into a new direction.

Biblical Inspiration. Read the biblical citations, each of which relates to today's theme.

Isaiah 11: 2

Ephesians 1:18

Notes:

Day 3/40 Calm as a River

"The ideal of calm exists in a sitting cat." --Jules Renard 1864-1910

What does "calm" mean? Calm refers to the absence of discord. Calm has two meanings, depending on what your perspective is. To be calm is both 'not to show anger, fear, or other strong feelings and emotions' and 'not to feel anger, fear, or other strong feelings and emotions'. Two very different concepts.

Our very strong emotions and feelings are not something we want to ignore; they are signals to us of deeply felt and often unconscious truths about ourselves and our lives. Feelings and emotions are a part of who we are, and to ignore or try to suppress them is not the best and certainly not the healthiest thing we can do.

How then do we approach life when others expect us to be calm or we expect ourselves to be, even in the midst of very difficult times? Rather than berating ourselves for what we don't feel or what we are not, use this retreat time to simply 'be enough'.

During the Retreat-in-Daily Life, the world that is happening in and around us. Nothing stops, nothing changes so that we can have more or less time. The movement of our lives is dynamic, and we carry forward whatever has happened, affected, or challenged us along the way. Forgetting about grief, anger, fear, frustration, or whatever is disturbing to you, can only be done when we are willing to befriend the hurt, loss, or pain that lies beneath emotions and feelings.

Befriending your feelings and emotions can be a very healthy thing. It is a normal experience to have strong feelings and emotions. During the retreat, you may notice that by becoming more mindful of feelings, one new grief may unlock unexpressed grief of the past. For example, when a pet dies, it often triggers other losses. Everything we experience is connected, and the chain of our emotions is no exception.

Pleasure, a nice emotion, also links to others pleasures. And sometimes to other emotions that are not so pleasant. Sometimes we do not allow ourselves pleasure because we link pleasure to some experience in the past that convinced us somehow that we were not worthy of being happy or loved again.

Consider what is arising into your awareness. What emotions or feelings are you having a hard time either facing or befriending? How you need to feel calmer? What are the overriding emotions or feelings, or lack thereof, that seem to be most obvious to you at this time? What strong feelings and emotions might require your attention?

It is a good thing to be able to look grief in the face and let our tears flow. It is good to be able to take anger's hand and seek a way to release and express it in a manner that does not cause harm or increase our rage. It is a much-needed gift to feel what we feel, to have emotional reactions, and to express our feelings and emotions, for that is where Calm lives—beneath that which is flooding our minds, hearts, and bodies with feelings that have gone unattended.

Letting go of the idea that you need to stop feeling something you feel, is a healthy acknowledgment of what you need to befriend.

Just for today, stop fighting yourself. Surrender and trust that the Divine Light that is within you is infused by the Divine Love that guides, guards, and helps comfort and heal all wounds and losses. When you feel your anger rising, ask yourself, "What is it I am fighting?" When you feel the urgent need to intervene or fix something about yourself or someone else, ask yourself, "What would happen if I let this just be?"

Words of Inspiration.

Calm: To not show or not feel nervousness, anger, or other strong feelings.

"To not show focuses on how we appear to be to others.

To not feel focuses on how we actually feel."

Synonyms: serenity, tranquillity, equanimity, imperturbability, equability, placidness, placidity, impassiveness, impassivity, dispassion, phlegm, stolidity

Origin: From the Greek word, karma meaning 'in the heat of day'

"Life is a series of natural and spontaneous changes. Don't resist them; that only creates sorrow. Let reality be reality. Let things flow naturally forward in whatever way they like." Lao Tau

"Be calm. God awaits you at the door."

— Gabriel García Márquez, Love in the Time of Cholera

"Peace is present right here and now, in ourselves and in everything we do and see. Every breath we take, every step we take, can be filled with peace, joy, and serenity. The question is whether or not we are in touch with it. We need only to be awake, alive in the present moment." — Thích Nhât Hạnh

"Change what cannot be accepted and accept what cannot be changed." — Reinhold Niebuhr

"We are but a speck in the Universe
Oh, but what a lucky speck to be..." — Kehinde Sonol
Serenity is found when wading into it."

— Rodney Ross, The Cool Part of His Pillow

Biblical Inspiration:

Psalm 46: 1-11

Isaiah 41:10, 13

Just for Today. Notice how CALM comes and goes in and out of your life throughout the day, Notice when you feel the urge to do something that may or may not be necessary. Just for today, be a mindful a little more often than usual.

Take a slow walk (slow down your pace from your normal gait).

Do things a little more slowly. Walk more slowly, wash a dish more slowly. Take your time and use it differently

Notes:

Day 4/40 Home is Where the Heart Is

To be home is to be where you belong. To be home is to return to that place where you can be yourself and feel safe, relaxed, and at peace. The dwelling we live in is part of what makes us feel at home, but today consider that place within you that is where you find peace. That place where you return from where your mind, your journeys, and your emotions take you. Where do you feel at home?

Yesterday, we reflected on the concept and experience of CALM. Another longing we have, and an essential need, is for home, a place where we belong. Our contemporary world has created a fluidity of life that is unlike any time before in our history. For ages sailors, explorers, and adventurers sought to discover what was beyond the familiar, beyond what one knew or understood. Now due to such rapid advances in technology, communication, and transportation, we move about the planet en masse.

Millions on our planet have been displaced from their homes. Others have sought to make home in new lands. Circumstances sometimes define the journey; choice defines it at other times. Reflect on the major circumstances that have taken place in your life—the ones that have opened a new door in a new direction. Bring to mind the choices you have made that have changed your life and have redefined what home means to you.

Home originally meant a permanent place where one lives, and/or where one originates from. The connotation, and more apt in many cases for what home has come to mean to us, is the place where one feels connected and where one belongs.

One friend comes to mind as I write this. She had been living on the Northern Island in New Zealand, happily ensconced in a high level job as an academic and theologian. She talked about simplifying her life, and decided to give up her position and return to parish life on the Southern Island, where her family is from. Many thought her choice odd, but that did not deter her. So she moved. Within a year or two of her relocation, the first of two devastating earthquakes struck her new home and community. Suddenly, without warning, her life changed.

Her new position as local parish minister and social service liaison put her life on an entirely new track. Who would have imagined that making a choice (surely with a different set of expectations than what she found), would put her in the perfect place to minister to, and help in the healing of the devastation that has taken place in Christ Church NZ.. She had joined others in helping recover and begin to rebuild from the devastation when a second even more destructive and deadly quake took place. Surely this is not something she wanted nor could foresee happening. Yet she along with so many from this community, have been dealing with the adversity and are marked by their experiences.

In my life I have known many survivors of war, oppression, and trauma. It does not surprise me that amidst great tragedy we discover gifts. For to survive some of the most difficult conditions, experiences, and struggles, people have to find some kernel of meaning, some light to keep hope alive, and something or someone to live for. When we suffer greatly, we have the opportunity to fall in love with who we are and what our life is.

If we are constantly railing against what is, always wishing for more or hoping for some magic genie to make everything better, we miss being wholly engaged in what is calling us right where we are. There is not one person I can think of who doesn't have some condition or situation that others would find unbearable. Yet, we bear. We put one foot in front of the other, and carry on. We keep trying, or keep answering the call. We keep seeing one more thing to be taken care of, or we learn new ways of expressing ourselves.

So how does one find what Gerald May calls, the gifts in the garbage when our lives do not fit some imaginary ideal? Where find the blessings amid devastation or after when experiencing great loss or trauma? How do we make sense of that causes suffering?

Give yourself time today to reflect on what you are in love with about your life, about yourself, about those in your life. Give yourself time to reflect on what you can do to ease another's burden a bit, or to help someone pick up the pieces from the devastation of their lives. Give yourself some time to notice when and where you feel at home, and notice whether you are in love with the way you are living. Be kind to yourself, and avoid judging. Just notice where your love dwells.

Words of Inspiration:

"Love cannot be a means to any end. Love does not promise success, power, achievement, health, recovery, satisfaction, peace of mind, fulfillment, or any other prizes. Love is an end in itself, a beginning in itself. Love exists only for love. The invitation of love is not a proposal for self-improvement or any other kind of achievement. Love is beyond success and failure, doing well or doing poorly. There is not even a right and wrong way. Love is a gift. One can never be proud of being in love. One can only be grateful." — Gerald G. May

"you are not too old
and it is not too late
to dive into your increasing depths
where life calmly gives out
it's own secret"
— Rainer Maria Rilke

"May what I do flow from me like a river, no forcing and no holding back, the way it is with children."
— Rainer Maria Rilke

"Trees are sanctuaries. Whoever knows how to speak to them, whoever knows how to listen to them, can learn the truth. They do not preach learning and precepts, they preach, undeterred by particulars, the ancient law of life.

A tree says: A kernel is hidden in me, a spark, a thought, I am life from eternal life. The attempt and the risk that the eternal mother took with me is unique, unique the form and veins of my skin, unique the smallest play of leaves in my branches and the smallest scar on my bark. I was made to form and reveal the eternal in my smallest special detail.

A tree says: My strength is trust. I know nothing about my fathers, I know nothing about the thousand children that every year spring out of me. I live out the secret of my seed to the very end, and I care for nothing else. I trust that God is in me. I trust that my labor is holy. Out of this trust I live." —Herman Hesse.

From Anne of Avonlea, by L.M. Montgomery:

"After all," Anne had said to Marilla once, "I believe the nicest and sweetest days are not those on which anything very splendid or wonderful or exciting happens but just those that bring simple little pleasures, following one another softly, like pearls slipping off a string."

"Home wasn't a set house, or a single town on a map. It was wherever the people who loved you were, whenever you were together. Not a place, but a moment, and then another, building on each other like bricks to create a solid shelter that you take with you for your entire life, wherever you may go."
— Sarah Dessen, What Happened to Goodbye

"God is Love."

Metaphysical definition of love: "Love is metaphysically defined as the prime cause of cosmos and opponent of chaos, the pre-eminent, transcendent uni–force in the universe uniting all being and creation together which in its ontological, highest earthly manifestation, is the root life force permeating and guiding all life toward life's greatest transcendental advancements, wholeness and primacy."

Just for today, be still and allow yourself to sink into being at home wherever you are. Watch your thoughts, and reign those in that take your and your energy on wild rides into negative scenarios or fantasies. Watch to see how often you travel into some unknown future time or start calculating your next task before you are finished with the one at hand. Watch how powerful your mind can be in taking you away from home, without even leaving its confines.

Just for today, spend some time meditating, praying, or contemplating one small step you can take to be more compassionate. Think of something you can release in your own life that would benefit someone in need. Letting go of perfectly good clothes that you don't wear.
Be your own Sunshine Division, and maybe join with friends or neighbors in setting up a way to help those in your community in need.

Just for today, fall in love with your home and with those who make a home in your heart.

Biblical Inspiration:

Song of Solomon 8:4-7

Matthew 22:34-40

In biblical scriptures, home is referred to when anyone has completed their task, their journey. It is the destination to which everyone returns at the end of day, and when all the worldly tasks are tended to, home is the destination. What is HOME to you?

Notes:

Today when I woke up, I found several messages from people who expressed a longing that is universal—the longing for peace and an end to violence and tragedy wrought on one human by another. Deep within each of us is an essential desire and hope for peace and love. As you enter deeper into this retreat-in-daily life, do so with a heart open to receiving the gifts of joy, peace, and love that are abundant in the Universe.

Go to that place where you allow yourself to receive inspiration. Go to that place within that allows you to feel the depth of your emotions. Go to that place where you are willing to surrender yourself to the Goodness within each of yourself—within each of us. Be receptive to the Universal outpouring of Love. And let your heart be open and receptive to that flow.

Take some time today to dip yourself into the cleansing waters of music, art, nature, and let yourself connect to that which nourishes, inspires, and touches you.

Let yourself be vulnerable to feeling where you need greater connection to the Sacred. All you need to do is get out of the way, and let the Holy fill you with that beauty of love. Consider how you might give up the struggle for d a while, and let the life you have be enough? Let yourself feel what it is to be grateful. And show that love and gratitude in simple small acts of loving kindness.

Find a kernel of truth that moves you forward and comforts you even when you mind won't be quiet or your life seems to be out of control.

For those times when hope seems hard to come by, have courage.

Words of Inspiration:

"If seeds in the black earth can turn into such beautiful roses, what might not the heart of the human become in its long journey toward the stars?" — Gilbert Keith Chesterton
"No one's life should be rooted in fear. We are born for wonder, for joy, for hope, for love, to marvel at the mystery of existence, to be ravished by the beauty of the world, to seek truth and meaning, to acquire wisdom, and by our treatment of others to brighten the corner where we are." —Dean Koontz

"The longest day must have its close--the gloomiest night will wear onto a morning. An eternal, inexorable lapse of moments is ever hurrying the day of the evil to an eternal night, and the night of the just to an eternal day." —Harriet Beecher Stowe

"What oxygen is to the lungs,
such is hope to the meaning of life."—Emil Brunner

Expectancy speeds progress. Therefore, live in a continual state of expectancy. No matter how much good you are experiencing today, expect greater good tomorrow. Expect to meet new friends. Expect to meet new and wonderful experiences. Try this magic of expectancy and you will soon discover a dramatic side to your work which gives full vent to constructive feeling."
—Ernest Holmes

Biblical Inspiration:

Psalms 3:2-6

Job 11: 8-9

From the Prophet Isaiah: 40:31

1 John 4:18

Galatians 5:5

Spend some time today connecting with the music or art, with the natural world or with your inner reveries, to find some places where you rediscover hope and peace.

Notes:

Day 6/40 Looking for Light

Today reflect on what lightens your load in life. What lightens your way? What do your struggles shine a light on?

Our experiences, of both light and darkness, profoundly affect our outlook on life, our emotional and psychological well being, and our appreciation and connection with ourselves, others, and the Great Mystery. When we experience the dark night of the soul, we have a lack of Light, and we long for something to connect us to something that will illuminate that still small corner of our hearts and souls, allowing us to come back to life and light again.

Loss, grief, and depression are all affected by Light or lack thereof. We lose the light of someone who filled up the darkness for us. We long for the light of someone's eyes after the lights have gone out. In depression and anxiety, we barely have room for light, but need it desperately.

Where do you need Light?

What are the ways you seek Light in your life?

Suggestions: Get out of your comfortable, cozy nest, and explore the natural world. Get a different perspective, and let some light enter your experience in new ways. That may be in reading something new, listening to a new piece of music, or walking along a path with your focus new looking for nuances of Light.

Pay attention to your sense throughout the day, noticing where you feel light, and when you don't.

What ignites the spark of Light within you?

What do you radiate from the Light within you?

Words of Inspiration:

Leonard Cohen, songwriter, singer, author, "There is a crack in everything, that's how the light gets in."

Edward Teller. "When you get to the end of all the light you know and it's time to step into the darkness of the unknown, faith is knowing that one of two things shall happen; either you will be given something solid to stand on, or you will be taught to fly."

Og Mandino. "I will love the light for it shows me the way, yet I will endure the darkness for it shows me the stars."

Catherine Al-Meten. "Winter makes stargazing and sunrises possible for those like me who rise with the Light."

And from one of my greatest explorers of darkness, Sir Arthur Conan Doyle: "It may be that your are not yourself luminous, but that you are a conductor of light. Some people without possessing genius have a remarkable power for stimulating it."

Meditation on Light.

"Phosphorescence. Now there's a word to lift your hat to...to find that phosphorescence, that light within, that's the genius behind poetry," (Emily Dickinson). That is indeed the genius behind Life.

If we only ever look for the Light on sunny days, we will miss the intensity and depth of Light on days like today, when the gloom has set in and the rains are falling.

Light is such a powerful word and part of our lives. We use this word to describe so much. We "see the light" when something becomes clear to us. We "light a fire" when we set something into motion. We "light up" when someone we love calls, walks in the room, or when we hear that person's voice. We might be told to "lighten up" when we get too ponderous and serious about life. We describe our connection with the Divine as receiving the Light, or some use Light as a synonym for God. We talk about the 'light at the end of the tunnel' to refer to hope. We feel 'lighter' when a burden has been lifted or when we feel some kind of relief. We use this concept, Light, as a symbol and metaphor in much of our speech and writing.

Light illuminates us in some way. Physically, the light eliminates the darkness so you can see where you are going. Light from the Full Moon lights up the sky and everything under the Sun. The Sun itself has given us life through its light, and our Earth is part of the Sun's family. We orbit on the axis of our earthly home, moving from night/dark to day/light going in and out of the Sun's rays in the endless cycle of light and dark. Emotionally, we feel lighter at times when we are in touch with our positive feelings--happiness, joy, peace, calm, love. Spiritually and in other ways, light is used to refer to understanding, to coming out of darkness or loss to see life through a lightness of being.

It's no wonder that we use light and lack of light/dark in how we describe all different experiences of our lives. What does light mean to you, and how do you use? Focus on light as you notice it where you may not have noticed it before. Watch the way the light in the clouds change on a rainy day. Watch how the Sun travels across the sky from morning until night, and notice how you are affected by the light and the changes throughout the day. In the North in winter, we experience the darkest days of the year. Each day ends earlier and brings the darkness ever earlier, and each night goes on longer. We wake in the dark, come home from work in the dark, or stand and wait for buses or friends in the dark, in what was only a couple of months ago, afternoon. We do with less light, and it changes the way we feel and live. In Spring and Summer, the days steadily grow longer, and nights grow shorter. Throughout the year, we experience the changes in light and notice how it affects our moods, the way we live, and certainly how it affects our climate and lifestyle.

Light, used as a metaphor for our spiritual, intellectual, emotional, psychological, or physiological condition, is a strong part of our vocabulary. With that in mind, today's reflection is on how we understand Light. As the first week of this reflective journey is nearing completion, spend some time contemplating what lights your way--each day, in troubled times, in times of great hope, in times of confusion, and in times when expectations have become too much.

We all have times in our lives when life gets a little more difficult, and our outlook and attitude reflect aspects of ourselves that we'd rather not anyone see and we certainly would rather not feel.

Inspiration:

"Love is not consolation. It is Light." --Simone Weil

"The only whole heart is a broken one because it lets the Light in." --David Wolpe

"Light,
Light
the visible reminder of
 invisible Light." --t.s. eliot

"There will always be a door to the light." --Shiro Amano

Biblical Scriptures:

Matthew 5:14

Psalms 119: 105

Psalms 27:1

Psalms 119:130

Matthew 5:16

Notes:

Day 7/40 Creativity and Soul Connections

"Clouds come floating into my life, no longer to carry rain or usher storm, but to add color to my sunset sky." Rabindranath Tagore

Today dip your fingers, eyes, heart, and soul into color. Let your senses guide you to discover how color and creativity bring your world to life. Wassily Kandinsky, the great artist, said that "color directly influences the soul." How does color enter into your experience of spirituality? How do your senses awaken you and help you connect to your soulful center?

Color may be experienced through the arts--music, dance, painting, drawing, sculpting. Color fills our world, and we are composed of many colors, all of them vibrating and brilliant in the Light.

What colors are filling your life now? What colors brighten your mood, and which ones leave you feeling heavy and low? How does light, color, creativity, and art influence your spiritual journey at this point?

Just for today, take some time to dabble in something creative. Wrap a colorful scarf around your shoulders, or draped a beautiful piece of cloth on the table or over the back of the couch. Add some color to you life--color the cookies with food coloring, or arrange a dinner with color in mind. Appeal to all your senses in whatever you do today, to awaken yourself to the beauty, richness, and depth of your world.

Go for a walk, and gather some wild flowers or sprigs from the Cedar tree, Eucalyptus leaves, or Magnolia tree. Let yourself breathe in the aromas of the earth--salty sea air, musty muck and mire of the path to the river, fishy diesel smells of the harbor, or the fresh, pine smells of a mountain trail.

Enjoy letting yourself do something to express yourself without words. Let yourself dab some paint on a canvas. Sit and draw a scene in a restaurant or photograph your pets. Rearrange a space in your house to welcome in room for being creative and fill your life with colors that inspire you.

Words of Inspiration:

"Color is a power which directly influences the soul." Kandinsky

"Why do two colors, put one next to the other, sing? Can one really explain this? No. Just as one can never learn how to paint." --Pablo Picasso

"Color directly influences the soul. Color is the keyboard, the eyes are the hammers, the soul is the piano with many strings. The artist is the hand that plays, touching one key or another purposively, to cause vibrations in the soul." Kandinsky

"They sang the words in unison, yet somehow created a web of sounds with their voices. It was like hearing a piece of fabric woven with all the colors of the rainbow. I did not know such beauty could be formed by the human mouth." Anita Diament, author of The Red Tent.

"Let me, O, let me bathe my soul in colors; let me swallow the sunset and drink the rainbow."
Khalil Gibran

"Art is a collaboration between God and the artist, and the less the artist does, the better." Andre Gide

"Life is a spiritual dance and that our unseen partner has steps to teach us if we allow ourselves to be led. The next time you are restless, remind yourself it is the Universe asking 'Shall we dance?'"
Julia Cameron

"Creativity requires faith. Faith requires that we relinquish control." Julia Cameron

Biblical Inspiration.

1 Chronicles: 1-4

Psalms 149:3

1 Chroinicles 6: 31-32 "

Notes:

Week Two
Day 8/40 Deepening Where We Are

"The geographical pilgrimage is the symbolic acting out an inner journey. The inner journey is the interpolation of the meanings and signs of the outer pilgrimage. One can have one without the other. It is best to have both."
— Thomas Merton

A Retreat-in-Daily Life is a pilgrimage within. Sometimes we take a journey for pleasure, education, or to attend to something that happens at our destination. Sometimes during those journeys, amazing and spiritually enlightening experiences occur—events or connections that change us forever. Whatever your reasons for taking this journey, you will experience yourself in new ways.

While deepening your awareness of the Divine in your life you are also turning your attention toward how the details, crises, distractions, gifts, and opportunities are arising in and around you.

As you focus on deepening, consider the Hebrew words for hope. There are two words for hope. *Tiqvah* is the sense of eager anticipation or waiting. The word *ellipse* is the sense of confident expectation based on certainty. What is it that you are hoping for (in your life, this week, in some specific area of life, or in your own soul development)? What is it you have a sense of confident expectation about?

Consider today, what is deepening in your life. Consider where your journey has taken you, and contemplate the major turning points in your life. What are the events or experiences that have rocked your world? What choices did you make that changed the course of your life? How have you already grown, changed, or healed?

At this point in your life, what seem to be the main stumbling blocks? What are your greatest gifts and who are your strongest allies? What helps you hold yourself together when times are tough? Who do you support and feel a need to help along the way?

On a pilgrimage, we need to garner our strength for the journey. We need good and trustworthy allies to walk and explore with. Take some time today to consider how far you have come, and what and who has been your greatest comfort. How has your experience of the Sacred grown, and what do you seek at this point in your spiritual life? How are your dreams, desires, daily life experiences, and relationships pointing you toward the journey your soul seeks?

Words of Inspiration:

"Not all those who wander are lost." J.R. Tolkien

"The most fulfilling adventures happen when you start your journey without knowing where you're going, because only then are you free to experience the unexpected detours you're meant to take."
— A.J. Darkholme

"Hope is a waking dream." Aristotle

Sometimes, reaching out and taking someone's hand is the beginning of a journey. At other times, it is allowing another to take yours."
— Vera Nazarian

Biblical Inspiration. Read the follwoing biblical passages, each of which relates to today's theme.

Jeremiah 29:11

Hebrews 11:1

Psalm 94:19

Isaiah 43:2

2 Corinthians 4:16-18

Psalm 34:18

Just for today, be grateful for the life you have, and for all you have been gifted with. Just for today, honor the journey you have chosen. Just for today, be still and acknowledge the gifts that are already yours.
Notes:

We dream of having a routine that fits a peaceful, serene lifestyle, and yet how often do we live a life that fits that dream? Some days you may feel more in the groove than on other days. Other days feel like you're slogging through the mud.

What about one day makes it more or less difficult than another? I have no answer to that, I just know that what seemed this morning like an easy task, turned into a day-long trudge through that proverbial sludge.

Just for today, be mindful of when you feel content with whatever is going on, regardless of how it fits into or upsets your plans or dream for perfection. Just for today, be glad of what is demanded of you, of what you demand of yourself, and what you have been able to do or haven't yet finished.

Notice the little unexpected gifts that come your way—a smile, an unexpected letter or phone call, or the sight of a bird outside your window.

Just for today, take a break now and enjoy the beauty of your own soul and energy. I think today of family and friends whose life journeys and toil have ended, and wonder if they wouldn't be satisfied for just one more day of being bone weary from doing what they loved?

Words of Inspiration:

"Toil without song is like a weary journey without an end." H.P. Lovecraft

William Shakespeare knew.
SONNET 27

Weary with toil, I haste me to my bed,
The dear repose for limbs with travel tired;
But then begins a journey in my head,
To work my mind, when body's work's expired:
For then my thoughts (from far where I abide)
Intend a zealous pilgrimage to thee,
And keep my drooping eyelids open wide,
Looking on darkness which the blind do see:
Save that my soul's imaginary sight
Presents thy shadow to my sightless view,
Which, like a jewel hung in ghastly night,
Makes black night beauteous and her old face new.
Lo, thus, by day my limbs, by night my mind,
For thee, and for myself, no quiet find.

Biblical Inspiration:

Proverbs 16:3

Isaiah 40:31

Ecclesiastes 2:24

Notes:

Crossroads and Turning Points: Standing at Choice

In every journey, indeed in each day's routine, we reach points of choice. One road may end and leave us wondering which way to turn. A crossroads presents us with an opportunity to make a choice. Some of our choices are great turning points, leading us into entirely new directions.

Just for today, consider the journey you are taking in your life. What does your daily routine look like? How does it nurture and support you? How do you nurture and support others? What is getting most of your energy and attention?

Just for today reflect on the crossroads you might be facing. What decisions loom before you? What seems to have reached a dead end or impasse? How are you being presented with new opportunities? What stops you from moving towards something that is healthier, more affirming, or perhaps more rewarding and fulfilling?

Just for today, consider how you are growing, changing, and developing. What is growing stronger within you? What turning points have been the most important in your life?

Notice what is moving and vibrating within you. Notice that which causes you to tremble or shake, to feel edgy or impatient, and allow yourself to breathe deeply. Use your own breath and breathing to help yourself calm down and find a little more inner peace.

Allow yourself to practice refocusing your attention from what is upsetting you to what is calming and grounding. Take a walk. Open the window and breathe in some fresh air. Take time to sit and have a cup of tea. Meet a friend for
coffee, or take a friend some soup or a bouquet of herbs from your garden. Use the simple gifts of life to connect yourself to the higher, more Divinely inspired nature of your being.

Sometimes we think a spiritual journey has to be done away from and above the messiness of our lives. Just for today, let yourself slosh though life's messiness. Embrace the busy-ness, befriend the chores left undone, and receive the gifts that are yours. Befriend the idea that you are enough. You have done enough for now. And before you move to the right or the left. Before you choose between one direction and another. Give yourself some time to rest, recuperate, reflect, and wait for inspiration that opens your eyes and heart to the way of your soul journey.

Words of Inspiration.

"In every life there is a turning point. A moment so tremendous, so sharp and clear that one feels as if one's been hit in the chest, all the breath knocked out, and one knows, absolutely knows without the merest hint of a shadow of a doubt that one's life will never be the same."
—Julia Quinn

"Each day is a new beginning. You can start fresh, anticipating what today will bring. Or you can just settle for yesterday's doubts, fears, or worries. Which road will you take? Do you take the path to the clear present or the the shadows of the past?"
— Eve Evangelista

"When at a crossroads, my father was fond of saying "go with your gut." "Intuition," he said, "always has our best interests at heart." It is a voice that can tell us who is friend and who is foe…Which ones to hold at arm's length…And which ones to keep close. But too often, we become distracted by fear, doubt, our own stubborn hopes, and refuse to listen."
— Emily Thorne

"Do not follow where the path may lead. Go, instead, where there is no path and leave a trail."
— Ralph Waldo Emerson

"Twenty years from now you will be more disappointed by the things you didn't do than by the ones you did do. So throw off the bowlines. Sail away from the safe harbor. Catch the trade winds in your sails. Explore. Dream. Discover." — Mark Twain

Biblical Inspiration:

Proverbs 16:16

Jeremiah 6:16

Proverbs 8.

Isaiah 49:11
Notes:

Day 11/40   Engaging, Embodying, and Embracing the Dance of Life

On this eleventh day of our Retreat-in-Daily Life, our journey takes us deeper into engaging with others, awakens us to the gifts of our embodied experiences, and calls for us to embrace the dance of Life.

Today a memory came flooding back to me from a time long ago when as a young woman, pregnant with my first child, I sat on a bench in a courtyard on the campus of the University I was attending, and realized that I was part of a beautiful, cosmic dance of life. Everyone moving towards me and away from me was a part of the Dance. The trees, recently planted in their concrete bunkers, were busily treeing the best they could. The sky was blue with a few scattered clouds, and as I sat, I could feel my deep connection to the Cosmic dance of life, to my Creator, and to everyone and everything that was. Part of the Divine Whole.

We are each expressions of the Divine Source, embodied in a unique experience of life. Each with gifts and talents, different experiences and challenges, and each of us at different stages of life. Whatever else you do today, take some time to appreciate the world around you. Engage in the beauty and surprises of the natural world. Gaze at stars, watch the Sun's path across the sky, or the clouds like ships, rolling across the ocean of sky. Feel the wind blow through your hair, and listen to it howl through the trees or down the canyon of skyscrapers in the City.

Just for today, be mindful and present with each person you encounter. Seek connection of kinship with each soul. Listen. Wait to speak. Let words unfold and sink in before rushing to fill in space. Let yourself remain still and receptive to others. Look for a metaphor for the life you are living. Find some meaning in what you consider ordinary.

Just for today, slow your pace and take your time doing whatever is needed.

Just for today, be still. In each moment, pause and turn your attention to how that divine spark within you directs your eye, your feet, your thoughts, your heart, and your intention.

Just for today, listen to you intuition and your body. Honor both as key elements of your being, meeting simple needs with ease and joy.

Words of Inspiration.

"When we fear what other people think about us, we are frequently more focused on 'being interesting' and less focused on 'taking an interest.' That's why many people talk a great deal when they are anxious and why many people never feel heard. If both people and conversation are trying to be interesting, there is no one left to genuinely listen." — John Yokoyama,

"We have not come here to take prisoners
But to surrender ever more deeply
to freedom and joy.

We have not come into this exquisite world
to hold ourselves hostage from love. Run, my dear,
from anything that may not strengthen
your precious budding wings,

Run like hell, my dear,
from anyone likely to put a sharp knife
into the sacred, tender vision
of your beautiful heart.

We have a duty to befriend
those aspects of obedience
that stand outside of our house
and shout to our reason
"oh please, oh please
come out and play."

For we have not come here to take prisoners,
or to confine our wondrous spirits,
But to experience ever and ever more deeply
our divine courage, freedom,
and Light!—Hafiz

"Unconditional"

The breeze at dawn has secrets to tell you.
Don't go back to sleep.
You must ask for what you really want.
Don't go back to sleep.
People are going back and forth across the door sill
Where the two worlds touch.
The door is round and open.
Don't go back to sleep. —Rumi

Biblical Inspiration:

Genesis 18:1-33

1 John 3:18

Isaiah 11: 1-2

1 Corinthians 12: 8-10

Notes:

Last night during a restorative yoga class (that's the quiet, reflective type of yoga), a huge storm rocked the little wooden building where we were seeking 'inner peace' by the river. The louder the wind and rain got, the greater my anxiety and inner turmoil roiled up to the surface of my consciousness. As our instructor calmly guided us to center in on a quiet place within, my own quiet place within seemed to have disappeared. What arose instead was the compelling thought that I needed to acknowledge something that was going on inside that I had tried to just 'live with'. By the end of class, I found I had been graced with some insight that I might otherwise not have noticed.

Being connected to the collective energy of the Universe and to the world around us and the people and conditions in it, means that we are caught up in the energy of the world. Serenity, inner peace, and indeed peace of any kind, exist in spite of not in place of the turmoil that we live with. Our own inner turmoil is not something we can or should gloss over or 'eliminate'. Turmoil, anxiousness, or other emotions signal to us that we need to pay attention to something that we haven't been.

The idea of doing a retreat-in-daily life came to me after going through the Jesuit's Spiritual Exercises while in graduate school at Marylhurst University. At the time I was teaching on three or four campuses, helping take care of my aging Father, attending graduate school, running a household, and holding on for dear life. It was an exciting time and it was a demanding and stressful at times as well. The Spiritual Exercises, based on Ignatian Spirituality and the guidelines of St. Ignatius, took over 9 months, and involved developing regular spiritual practices.

After the exercises, I began using many of the precepts I had learned through this experience and combined them with my own ideas about how to minister to those whose spirituality ran somewhere around the perimeters or outside the borders of traditional religious traditions.

Retreat-in-daily life was born out of wonderful experiences I had with two of my spiritual teachers/spiritual directors--Dr. Sr. Frances Madden, a professor of philosophy and Dr. Fr. Henri La Certe. Both now deceased, live on in my heart and soul, and in the lives of so many they both touched. Sr. Frances and I participated in the Spiritual Exercises together, and I asked her to be my spiritual director.

A renowned professor of philsophy, Sr. Frances was also my teacher and spiritual director. The pivotal point for starting the retreat-in-daily life was designing a series of spiritual direction session with Sr. Frances that would fit both our busy schedules, yet serve to be intense and deepening.

Before we met for the first session, I had a dream of being in a kayak with another person. We were going down a narrow, fast-moving river, that wove its way through a narrow ravine, and into the rapids of the river. We paddled madly, avoiding crashing into the rocky sides of the ravine, and made our way through the rapids into the stillness of a beautiful lagoon. In the lagoon, I dove into the river, shedding my military uniform, and digging deep into the sandy riverbed with my hands. I discovered beautiful shells, jewels, and hidden treasures, some of which I carried to the surface and onto the bank of the river, where I sat down and rested.

For the last twenty years, I have designed and led retreats and retreats-in-daily life on numerous occasions. Sometimes I have done so with dear friends and colleagues; other times, I have woven it into my own spiritual practice. For the past five years I have done an annual virtual retreat-in-daily life.

For today, reflect on your own story. Who do you say you are? To yourself, to others? We all have a story that, when we take time to reflect on it, helps us weave meaning into our lives, and helps us gain perspective on who we are, why we are experiencing whatever we are, and may even give us a little insight into where we are headed.

What are the Divine plans that are opening up in your life?What is falling out of the uncertainty, disappointment, or closed doors? How is your story unfolding in ways that have nothing to do with your plans?

Just for today, spend some time reflecting on some of the key elements of your own story.

What are some of the key turning points in your life?
Who are some of the teachers who have appeared on your path, and who have inspired and supported your journey?

What gifts have you found in the garbage of your life, and who and what has led you to find the magic within you?

Looking over your life, see if you can discover some of the patterns, ways you have of learning, and ways that the Divine reveals to you, the next best step or the door that is waiting to be opened. What is the story you are telling of your life?

Suggestions: Have some fun with this. Play. Act. Sing. Dance. Sculpt. Do whatever moves you to be and tell the story of you and your spiritual life journey. Use writing, music, painting, or storytelling (recording or telling someone), letter writing, or journaling to tell your story. Reflect. Reframe the story. String together some meaning, and set out a map of hidden treasures you would like to go in search of. Notice how the way you look at life has changed.

Words of Inspiration:

"After nourishment, shelter and companionship, stories are the thing we need most in the world."
— Philip Pullman

"The human species thinks in metaphors and learns through stories." --Mary Catherine Bateson

"There is no greater agony than bearing an untold story inside you." --Maya Angelou

"Stories are a communal currency of humanity." --Tahir Shah, in Arabian Nights

Scriptural Storytelling and Narrative:

One of my favorite ways to approach life and sacred texts is through the use of narrative and story telling.
Narrative is the attempt to retell the events of history, linking one event to another and giving a more or less realistic answer to the question: What happened to whom?

Storytelling is retelling what happened with the desire to give meaning and purpose to events, and to present a piece of a longer story or life. There are many types of storytelling, including parables, a choice used by Jesus in using metaphor to help people understand the complexities of life.

You can see where both run into the obstacle of truth. We recite our narratives and tell our stories from our own viewpoints, perspective, and with what information or recall we have. We also tell our stories for different reasons to different people.

One of my favorite ways to approach scripture is to find a story I love, say the Wedding at Cana, or Moses going out into the Wilderness. I read the story, and then retell the story from the viewpoint of someone or something in the story. This form of storytelling is called Midrash, and it is used to flesh out the meaning of a complex scripture. To look at what was happening as if you were there, and from one of the viewpoints. The point is to look for how differently people might have seen that experience and how it still might connect to something going on in our own lives.

Select one of your favorite biblical stories. For example, the Wedding at Cana, David and Goliath, Daniel in the Lion's Den, Jesus meeting the woman at the well. Reread the story, and the retell the story in your own words. Imagine you are present in the story, and tell the story from the viewpoint of someone who was there. Allow yourself to enter into this process, letting the story flow.

Ask yourself "what in my life is like this?"

Day 13/40   Cycles, Patterns, and Centering

When I first led this retreat-in-daily life, we observed a special date— 12/13/14, a sequential date that happens rarely. It is fun when we recognize sequential patterns and repetitive cycles that occur. I say 'fun' because it's interesting in a quirky way. Notice patterns and cycles that occur for you when you are on an upswing or down in the dumps. Notice how patterns repeat themselves at various times in your life, and consider how to be more in synch with your own rhythms.

As a young woman, when my Mother sensed I was struggling to understand the complexities of living fully aware of the spirit, mind, body connections and conflicts, she would explain to me that understanding God and the workings of life were like understanding a mathematical equation; perfect in its profound simplicity, profound in its depths. Just as my lack of understanding did not make God any less God, and the Divine Sacred any less beautifully laid out it its perfect plan. God was regardless of what I could or could not understand.

Being a philosopher at heart, I've always longed to understand the "whys" of life. What I have discovered along the way is that regardless of how long I search or how many roads I take to try to figures out the answers to my questions, I probably will not find all the answers. Indeed, I may find few, but what I have discovered are paths. Paths lined with symbols, signs, and sometimes warnings. paths blocked, and paths opened. Turns and twists on the trail. Seeming dead ends and sudden stops with no clear way ahead. And yet, here I am. And here you are. And we keep on going.

When doing deep spiritual work as we are, we become ever more aware of not only our own struggles but also the challenges of others on the path with us. One good friend is suffering, being without a home and feeling lost and without a path. When we reach these points on our journeys, we have the opportunity of discovering in very concrete, practical terms, just what is basic and essential for us.

Consider what is essential to you. Our breath. Having enough food and a place to sleep. Shelter from the storms, both physical and metaphoric. Support and companionship. Peace of mind, and ideas. Trust in our surroundings and trust in our ability to overcome. And trust in the fact that each of us is a Divine being in the perfect protection, love, and embrace of the Creator. At no time are we without the essentials of our soul, and so when we are without the basics or the assurance of where we belong, we have ourselves and our connection to the Sacred Source.

Make a list of all the gifts you have--talents, skills, experiences (even the bad ones), friends and family (even if they're no longer living or nearby), health, senses, a mind, ideas, hope, the ability to bake bread or take a walk. From the most basic and simple gifts, what about life has made you who you are and made you rich?

Use your ability to pray, meditate, swim, hike, walk, or run to get your energy lifted up. If you are exhausted by what you have been going through, take a break. Consider yourself on vacation for an hour, a day, this week. The world will not end if you take a nap. Your problems will be solved and your challenges will be overcome without your constant worrying or hyper-vigilance. Put on some music and dance and sing. Pick up your instrument and play. Smear your hands with paint and paint something on a blank piece of paper. Create some beauty.

Sometimes we need to start from the outside to get inner change to take place; other times it's the opposite. Change your story, and the way you are living it out. For example if I tell myself I have no home--and I have felt like this in the past--I can remind myself that my home is always within me and is always wherever I am in the world.

Describe what home is to you.
Contemplate.
- What can you do for someone or give someone that would release the places within you and your life that seem to be stuck?
- How have the choices you have made to rid yourself of bad situations or conditions, freed you and your energy to heal, grow stronger, and be receptive to new opportunities?
- How is the situation you feel trapped in or are struggling to deal with showing you something new about yourself?
- How is it revealing an opening, a door, or a new way
- How is the Divine pointing you in a new direction?

Our faith and beliefs are tested, not in the quiet of the mountaintop or during the times we find to get away. Our faith and beliefs are tested in real life situations; in the moments when life overwhelms and perplexes us.

Psychiatrist and Spiritual Director, Gerald May observed:

"The purest acts of faith always feel like risks. Instead of leading to absolute quietude and serenity, true spiritual growth is characterized by increasingly deep risk taking. Growth in faith means a willingness to trust God more and more, not only in those areas of our lives where we are most successful but also, and most significantly at those levels where we are most vulnerable, wounded, and weak."

Words of Inspiration.

"Give us grace for today; feed the famished affections."
--Mary Baker Eddy

"And Love is reflected in Love."

"My peace I give you." Christ Jesus

As love flows, love grows. A simple statement of about the physics of life and love.

Giving is a big part of our celebrations and our lives in general. Sometimes we give so much that we seem to exhaust ourselves. At other times it is hard to decide what to give or what we have to give. For many, it is a difficult time for giving is related to using our resources including money, time, energy, not to mention deciding on exactly what the perfect or appropriate gift would be.

Personally, when I'm well-rested, financially solvent, and feeling safe and secure, it seems easier for me to give. The problem comes in figuring out what I have to give when I'm worn out, low on funds, or feeling fearful and shaky about life. The idea that we have to be 'good enough' or 'have enough' to be worthy of giving to others is something that stems from a place of fear.

Remember that Divine Love and Intelligence are manifesting in our lives right now. God's rich abundance is not limited and finite. What stands in the way of realizing the richness of life are the false beliefs of lack. The Creator is our Source of all supply.

Meditation on God as the Source.

"We are ever renewing and we are the ever unfolding expression of God's love, infinite health, life, and energy. Rather than dwelling on what stops or blocks or slows us, recognize now how we are expressions of God's radiant love in body, mind, and spirit. And that we are expressing that radiant perfection now.

Whatever is not in accordance with our highest good, is fading from experience and is no longer a desire. That which is desirable and good, now fills my attention and affections. In Divine time and according to Divine Intelligence, good now fills us up.

Live in ceaseless gratitude, and needs will be met, desires fulfilled, and blocks will disintegrate. In gratitude, Divine Love is the guiding principle of life, opening doors, removing obstacles, and providing abundantly for all needs of all now. Filled with Love, we pour forth into all areas of our lives, the beauty, peace, compassion, love, and bounty that extends on in a continuous flow, endlessly.

God's Spirit of Love and Good is active and producing results now. There is nothing to fear. As we surrender to God, active in our lives, we receive our good. Divine intuition is now showing the way. Divine is working in us, through us, and through all concerned in all areas of our lives."

Remember, "There is not a place, there is not spot in all the world where God is not. Nothing in all the world to fear, for God is Love and God is here."

Enjoy the gift of Life, and the gift of Love. For as St. Francis of Assisi observed, "It is in giving that we receive."

"Gaudete in Domino semper" means rejoice in God always. The first lines of the Latin mass find their source in the Psalms.

In the Hebrew Scriptures, Psalms is the book entitled, Tehillim, meaning praises. Psalms is the first book in the Kituvim (the third section of the TANAKH (Torah, Nevaiim/Prophets, Kituviim/ Writings). The roots of the Abrahamic traditions, Judaism, Christianity, and Islam, all find their source in the traditions of the ancients.

To rejoice, to sing praises for the Divine is to express the love and gratitude for being part of the ongoing Divine Creation. As we discover, within our own lives, the miraculous unveiling of our deepest selves, and of the beauty and depth of those we know and love, we share in this Creative energy.

Love within you is released through your thoughts, feelings, words, actions, and presence with one another. By first recognizing your own innate capacity to love, we then allow ourselves to love and be loved in return. What does that look like in our lives?

The Source of Love has created you in the image and likeness of that Divine Love. The flame of love is lit within you; it does not depend on another to create that spark. As we express love, love reflects back to us, and we share our lives with one another, as we are. We are not at the mercy of others, conditions, or situations.

As we call on Divine Love to heal our woundedness, straighten out and adjust situations, and melt away situations or conditions that seem impossible for us to bear, we open ourselves to the activation of Love in every area of our lives. And we perpetuate the cycle of love by sharing our love with others.

Recognize how the Divine is working through you and your life to perform miracles. Thinking about miracles as I sit watching the morning sky fill with light, the birds begin the day's flights, and the sounds of life starting up again today, the promise of miracles is everywhere.

Sometimes we need to remind ourselves of how much love and good is within. One simple practices might help you strengthen your mindfulness practice.

The practice of Ahimsa is the practice of doing no harm. Do no harm to yourself through words, thoughts, and deeds. Do no harm to others as well. Our actions are shaped by what we know about ourselves, so just for today, pay attention to how you talk to yourself. What do you say about others? How do you talk about yourself? How do you love and affirm yourself, and see yourself as a loving, caring person?

Just for today, pay attention to how your thoughts, words, and deeds reflect your ability to love and be loved.

Another practice is called the examen of conscience. It is a form of prayer that comes out of the Ignatian tradition. The examen of conscience is a self-reflective prayer that can be done anywhere and at different times of the day. Some do this before going to sleep at night, others do it twice a day, once around mid-day and then again before going to sleep. When I am very busy, I like the break in the middle of the day to take time to be more reflective and still. Whenever you choose to do it, is fine.

1. Begin by becoming aware of being in God's Presence. Know the Creator' concern for you, and that Divine Presence within and around you. Let yourself feel that connection. Notice what how that happens. One day the connection may come through music, on another through a conversation or laughter with a friend. How do you feel God's Presence now?

2. Spend some time looking over the day's gifts with gratitude. This is particularly helpful when you're tired, frustrated, or feeling unproductive. Notice the gifts of space, time, quiet, gaps in a heavy schedule, or whatever it is that is a gift. Notice how something that might look like a problem, delay, or crisis can be a gift in the garbage. What about a problem, challenge, or situation may be turned into a gift. At least a part of it. For example, if I lose a job, I suddenly have more time.

Notice what you wish or pray for, and notice what happens when you get what you want. The way our prayers are answered, it seems, sometimes looks like a disaster, not a gift. However, in examining those areas of our lives, we need to find meaning and lessons that are helping us grow or resolve something that is causing us grief of pain. Pain and grief diminish bit by bit through the infusion of small acts of kindness, tiny drops of love, and little gestures and acts that restore light and life to those areas of ourselves that need Love the most.

3. The third step in the examen of conscience is to ask that the Divine, Holy Spirit be with you to guide, guard, and show you what needs to understood, seen, or done. The Holy Spirit within us directs our actions and attitudes, and guides us to be more authentic, honest, and receptive to the flow of love. As you reflect, ask what it is that you need to learn or to grow in.

4. Review the day. Notice the areas of the day that were uplifting, rewarding, and fulfilling. Notice those areas of the day that leave you feeling unfinished, upset, or discouraged. "Ask what you were involved in and who you were with, and review your hopes and hesitations. Many situations will show that your heart was divided—wavering between helping and disregarding, scoffing and encouraging, listening and ignoring, rebuking and forgiving, speaking and silence, neglecting and thanking. Remember, this is not a time to dwell on your shortcomings; rather, it is a gentle look with

Divine guidance at how you have responded to God's gifts. It is an opportunity for growth of self and deepening your relationship with God. Notice where you acted freely—picking a particular course of action from the possibilities you saw. See where you were swept along without freedom. What reactions helped or hindered you?

5. Spend some time in prayer, talking to and listening and watching for the Divine to speak to you. God communicates with each of us in the ways that meet us where we are. However you feel, experience, or understand the sacred in your life, allow yourself to grow in love and understanding. Find gratitude, joy, and love and rejoice.

Inspiration:

"Resolve never to criticize or downgrade yourself, but instead rejoice that you are fearfully and wonderfully made."— Elizabeth George

"There is not one blade of grass, there is no color in this world that is not intended to make us rejoice."
— John Calvin

Biblical Biblical Scriptures:
Psalms 84: 1-4

Deuteronomy 12:7

Matthew 2:10

Romans 5:2
Notes:

"Comfort, comfort my people says our God....A voice of one calling:'In the wilderness prepare the way for the Lord; make straight in the desert a highway for our God."
" From the prophet Isaiah...40: 1, 3.

The people of the Abrahamic traditions (Judaism, Christianity, Islam) are like all other holy seekers, wilderness people. Our inner journey is a wilderness experience, part of our sacred journey.

The wilderness is a liminal place-an in-between place, neither home nor at the destination. Wilderness is a place an uncultivated, uninhabited, and inhospitable region. The wilderness is a place that has been abandoned or neglected. It is an uncharted, unexplored, or un mapped region. It also refers to a bewildering or confusing situation.

In our lives, we reach points or have wilderness experience. Those times when our experiences feel like we are entering vast, uncharted territory. Places, conditions, experiences, or phases of life that seem overwhelming new, strange, and awesome. By awesome I refer to the original meaning of the word--to be filled with awe.

What about your life is or has been like a wilderness experience ?

Where do you find the wilderness experience? How do you experience the Divine Presence in the wilderness?

While we are in the wilderness, we are in a place of exposure. We may be exposed to heat or cold or lack of water. We may be exposed to fears and anxieties. We meet ourselves and our Creator in the wilderness. Sometimes like Christ Jesus, we are tempted in the wilderness. At other times it is the only place we truly feel we know the Divine. And for others like St. Theresa of Avila, it is the only place where we know ourselves.

Just for today, allow yourself some time to explore the wilderness. Explore it by going outdoors, going for a hike, walking along the beach, sailing out on the ocean, or wandering some place that allows you time to be alone.

Just for today, enter into the wilderness places within yourself, and allow yourself to simply be at peace with all the questions, all the uncharted territory, and seek a piece of comfort and calm.

Just for today, think back to other times when you experienced the wilderness, and recall what lifted and sustained you.

What, today, do you need to sustain you? How are you affirming life and the mysteries yet unsolved? What is the gift today, that speaks most to your heart?

Inspiration:

"The wilderness holds more questions than we have yet learned to ask." -Nancy Wynne Newhall

"We are part of the Earth and the Earth is part of us. All things are bound together. All things connect. What happens to the Earth happens to the children of the Earth. Man [humans] has not woven the web of life. A human is but one thread of of that web. Whatever we do to the web, we do to ourselves." -Chief Seattle

"Only by going alone in silence, without baggage, can one truly get into the heart of the wilderness." -John Muir

"Climb the mountains and get their good tidings. Nature's peace will flow into you as sunshine flows into the trees. The winds will blow their own freshness into you and the storm their energy. And cares will fall off like autumn leaves." --John Muir

"Wilderness is not a luxury, but is a necessity of the human spirit. If you look throughout history...the central epiphany of every religious traditions always occurs in the wilderness." -Robert Kennedy

"We are all travelers in the wilderness of this world, and the best we can find in our travels is an honest friend." --Robert Louis Stevenson

For the ancients as for us, the wilderness was a place of where God's Spirit came to them most exquisitely and intimately. It is the point of transformation when we are at our most vulnerable place. Open to receiving the gifts of Spirit.

Notes:

"When we are no longer able to change a situation, we are challenged to change ourselves."
--Victor Frankl

Questions and struggle are part of the process of spiritual discernment. All these question that we struggle with from time to time, have to do with how we develop, grow, and come to a deeper understanding of our relationship with the Divine, the Sacred, that which is Holy. We each approach this differently, have different traditions and beliefs, and change and grow differently as we make our spiritual journey of life.

Discerning how the Divine is present in us and our lives also varies for each of us. How do we discern God's Presence? In ancient times in the Holy Lands prophets foretold the coming of a prophet, a Messiah. Someone who would save the people and put an end to war, violence, and animosity of one group against another.   As my wise then 6-year old Granddaughter commented when I was explaining how Jesus came to show people how to live in peace, "Well," she said, "They didn't listen!" And, she was right.

However, what we had not yet talked about is that we can live in peace and act from love even when things aren't going well, even when people still suffer and use violence as a means to an end. How we do this is my working within our own lives to find the seeds of Love within us--- that God-given essence of who we are--that enables us to meet the challenges, overcome obstacles, and discover the way through our own personal wilderness experiences.

Discerning is allowing all sides of an issue to work their way up into our awareness. Sometimes we call this 'inner conflict' while at others we see this as a dilemma or a choice, or a path with no end or a problem with no solution. The inner struggles along with the ways those struggles manifest in our relationships, our experiences at work, with family, or in some other area of our lives, are the 'stuff' of discernment.

Rather than viewing conflict, indecision, disagreements, or dilemmas as the end of the world, let's look at this material of our lives as fabric to work with. What can we create out of the struggle, chaos, or conflict? The process of discernment allows us to look at what is happening in the light of day--not ignoring or denying the problems or situations, but seeing them as they are.

Once we have named an issue or recognized an area our lives that needs fixing, adjusting, or eliminated, we can then begin to sense the energy that trapped us in worry, fear, or anxiety releasing its hold on us. Part of discernment is the simple acknowledgement of what is before us.

The next step is knowing what power or control we have over the situation. For many things, we have little say in how someone else feels or acts. We do however, have a say over how we respond or react ourselves. Discernment is about weighing the pros and cons about how to handle a situation. The phrase, "choose your battles" comes to mind for many times we are so busy fighting against the flow of the tide that we create more of a struggle than we need to.

Discernment is about deciding about what we choose to engage with or not. We ask ourselves and the Creator, "What is the loving thing to do in this situation?" "What gives me life, and what drains the life from me" You have your own questions that help you determine the choices you make along your path. Discernment allows us to ask the questions and then wait for the answers.

And this is the tricky part, as many of us think we are the only one who chooses and decides. We strive to be in control not only of what we decide but also of how we receive what we desire and what form it takes. Discernment is part of this Divine process of letting ourselves relax in the Presence of the Holy. After all the debating and arguing and working out of decisions, how can we release our hold on our prayers, allowing ourselves to surrender to the Divine flow of holy energy ever unfolding in our lives?

Watching, listening for, and waiting for answers, for guidance, for understanding, and for signs to show us the way through our wilderness times, is the beautiful life journey of discernment. Watching how life unfolds when we're not holding on so tightly. Watching to see what is showing us answers. Listening to what words connect us to the Truth, or what words have given us answers or sound affirmation or support.

Just for today, listen to the questions arising within you.
Just for today, allow yourself to sit with the obstacles, struggles, problems, or dilemmas that are holding you prisoner. Is the struggle primarily outer (circumstances, others, conditions) or inner? Notice what is draining your joy, energy, and life?

Just for today, watch and listen for signs, symbols, synchronicities, or simple openings that allow you to feel the Presence of the Divine more closely. Just for today, expand your idea of what the Divine is to include more love, more joy, and greater safety.

Just for today, look at how your life is like that of the Prophet Jonah. For the next few days, we'll look at different parts of his journey, and even though our lives are not like his, there is something of truth in his story that touches each of us. In what ways is the metaphor of Jonah's spiritual journey like our own?

Just for today, reflect back on a similar time when you faced overwhelming and seemingly insurmountable odds. How was the Divine Presence active in that time? What made the difference and removed the obstacles? How is your strength and knowledge helping you now?

Just for today, listen with am open heart and mind, to what your dreams, intuition, life experiences, and minor and major incidents are showing you about your journey. In his book Man's Search for Meaning about his survival in a concentration camp, Victor Frankl wrote in, "Those who have a 'why' to live, can bear with almost any 'how'."

Getting to that 'why' is part of the discernment process that helps us make sense of what is happening in our lives.

Victor Frankl's words have had a major influence on me in my life. He has given us a way to deal with the trauma, violence, and turmoil that marks so much of modern life. Of course in ancient times, everyone thought they were living through the worst of times as well. It's what we do as humans, look for the best and worst in life. When going through the experience of being in deep shock during the First Gulf War, my friends got me to a doctor to help me through the debilitating and overwhelming experience of traumatic shock I was experiencing.

At the time there was little known about PTSD or trauma related to violence and war. Yet the one person who was considered a trauma therapist, was who I visited. The only words I recall that he said to me came directly out of Frankl's work. The person said to me, what you are experiencing is "An abnormal reaction to an abnormal situation [it] is normal behavior." The links between our experiences and the words spoken to us, the actions taken to aid and support us, and the strength and affirmation we experience are all part of how the Divine Presence is alive within our lives.

The old Deuteronomist put it so beautifully, we have a choice in life, and this is it. We can choose life, or we can choose death. Choose life! Just for today, regardless of the situation, choose life!

Words of Inspiration:

The first story is about God calling Samuel.

1 Samuel 3: 1-10

"If you come at four in the afternoon, I'll begin to be happy by three." — Antoine de Saint-Exupéry, The Little Prince

When we are preparing for holidays, vacations, turning point events (births, marriage) or undergoing difficulties (deaths, loss, illness, unexpected trauma), we often feel increased stress. During such times, we can use our spiritual practices to help us manage and cope with whatever comes our way.

Focus the power of your mind and your inner power to create perfect health, wealth, love, creative expressions, and ideas. Trust that the Divine has filled you with the ability to know and accept the gifts you possess—the qualities that are always with you for you are made in the image and likeness of God. Let Truth be revealed, and let healing take place through knowing the Truth. Create heaven right here and now in you, and with all your connections with others.

Acknowledge the good in others, holding a place for others to be who they are, and for you to be who you are. Do what your heart calls you to do, and discover how the Love within you continually expresses itself through you. Regardless of circumstances or conditons, Divine Love reigns—guiding, guarding, and protecting us. Divine Love is doing perfect work within and through us right now. Love

We all face those difficult places in our lives right now, with even more concern and need. For all the unhealed relationships and parts of ourselves, we pray for Divine Love's healing grace. Knowing the Truth—that Divine Love heals and soothes—is a prayer that can help us direct our minds in positive, loving, and healing ways. "Love melts situations that seem impossible", is a prayer that can be used as a mantra, to be repeated over and over. Our thoughts and words have power, and do result in change and movement.

When there is a need for Love, we know we have a ready supply within us. Speak words of love to yourself. Develop practices to maintain the calm within you, especially when you know you are entering into a difficult period. Know that you are protected and shielded from harm, and allow yourself to recognize your capacity to be open to receiving help, support, and love.

How do you prepare yourself for difficult times? How do you build up a supply of patience, with yourself and with others? What thoughts, words, attitudes, and actions are coloring the way you are viewing life? What joy can you find right now in this journey?

"When you bring forth what is within you, what you bring forth will save you." (Christ Jesus, Gospel of Thomas).

What you bring forth is there to be shared, regardless of the outcome. Let life unfold as it does, and allow yourself to simply be present. Once you have set you plans down, then the journey will unfold with many surprises, with some new lessons to be learned, and in the way that accomodates everyone on the path.

The more you are able to relax in the moment of whatever you are doing, the more you create the peace that knows no bounds right here and now. A simple drive to someone's home can become the special event of your season. A conversation that you have with a stranger or a good friend, can become the gift you needed. The act of preparing and packing can become a meditation in Love.

Disappointments, dead ends, or broken plans can become the heart of a gift found in forgiveness, grief, or loss. We experience life with all its ups and downs, and sometimes our disappointments and sorrows overshadow our ability to see how Love is present even when our hearts are broken. Be present with what your experiences are now, and be open and receptive to allowing Love to build up within you, heal the broken places, and fill in the spaces that need comfort and caring. Give with all your heart, and receive the blessings pouring out into your heart and soul.

Inspiration:
"Anticipation is sometimes more exciting than actual events."
— Ana Monnar

Sit down before fact as a little child, be prepared to give up every preconceived notion, follow humbly wherever and to whatever abysses nature leads, or you shall learn nothing. I have only begun to learn content and peace of mind since I have resolved at all risks to do this."
— Thomas Henry Huxley, Life and Letters of Thomas Henry Huxley - Volume 1

"A waiting person is a patient person. The word patience means the willingness to stay where we are and live the situation out to the full in the belief that something hidden there will manifest itself to us."
— Henri J.M. Nouwen

Try looking at your mind as a wayward puppy that you are trying to paper train. You don't drop-kick a puppy into the neighbor's yard every time it piddles on the floor. You just keep bringing it back to the newspaper."
— Anne Lamott, Bird by Bird: Some Instructions on Writing and Life

"Make your ego porous. Will is of little importance, complaining is nothing, fame is nothing. Openness, patience, receptivity, solitude is everything."
— Rainer Maria Rilke

"The hardest work begins in dry dock."
— Sam Wineburg

"All things are ready, if our mind be so."
— William Shakespeare

Scripture: The biblical Biblical Scriptures today have to do with recognizing our spiritual heritage and gifts, and being in Divine Presence always. The second reading is from Jonah, and details the account of his struggles deep in the belly of the whale. What in your life right now is like being lika Jonah—trapped in a seemingly impossible situation? How do these words speak to you today?

The Servant of the Lord

Isaiah 42: 1-10

Jonah's Prayer

Notes:

Years ago I dreamed of being in a kayak, riding the rapids through a set of windy, narrow river rapids. At this point in time many of us may feel like that's what we are doing...riding the rapids, holding on for dear life, as we navigate through the narrows hoping to avoid being capsized or dashed against the rocks. At times like these, it is vital to slow down in our thinking, breathe more deeply and slowly, and focus our attention on only what is essential and necessary for riding the rapids.

Journeys are full of moments when we have to readjust our priorities, and find ways to be more mindful and present at whatever point we are on. In my life, this looks like making time for breathers and putting a little distance on the urgencies that loom ahead. Today, after being up since before dawn, working on an article I needed to finish, I found myself overwhelmed with what I felt had to be done during the rest of the day. That is the point at which I decided to stop, take a break, and start dropping tasks from my long list of things to do.

Not everything is equally urgent, and when doing something that is normally relaxing becomes a stress producer, it is time to let it go. Taking time out to sit with a friend and catch up over a cup of coffee is how I gave myself permission today to get perspective on what was growing into a giant obstacle. We create so many challenges out of the fantasies we make up in our own mind. When I calculated all the 'what ifs' that were clogging my thought processes, I realized I was setting myself up for trouble. There is no reason that any of us need to make ourselves slaves to our own thinking.

Wouldn't it be just as simple to let ourselves relax into each situation instead of creating panic and disaster scenarios in our heads? And those of us who believe we are part of a Divine plan, how on earth do we get to be such control freaks when it gets down to the nitty gritty? Well, I do not have the answers, but I certainly notice when I'm doing this in my own life. So for today, I am focusing on one little step at a time, and on breathing with greater intention, and acting with ease. By allowing myself to be mindful in each moment, I experience the present rather than sending my mind and energy into some future 'what if' or back over 'why did that happen' trail.

Staying on the path involves being present at each step of the journey. And if my destination is clear and my plans are right, I will get to where I'm meant to be. Life has always worked this way, yet sometimes I send myself into fantasies that distract and waste both my time and energy. Fortunately, my life has taught me how to be more present than I might have been. Being a Mother and Grandmother, keep me very present and open to what is happening at each step of my life as Mother, Grandmother. There is no forcing things to be what they are not, nor is there any pushing those I love most to be something they are not. It's so simple.

With writing, it is essential that I stay completely present in order to complete even one small article, let alone listen to the inspiration for a poem or a call for something epic and profound.

As a photographer, I have learned to narrow my focus in on one single image or movement or expression that requires my being still, calm, and ready.

As a woman I have learned to know myself as I become different parts of myself. I have learned to love myself more as I get older, and have stopped fighting myself as much over what I expect or what others expect of me. I have learned who I am in different relationships and roles, and most importantly, who I am at any given time in the Divine scheme of things.

Life is dynamic. It is our nature. It is what we are composed of...living, moving, changing particles, waves, idea, expressions, beliefs, thoughts, memories, dreams, hopes, and desires. All swirling and yet coming together in the perfect expression of who we each are. We are each a divine masterpiece, being and doing exactly what we are meant to be and do.

Just for today, spend some time exploring your personal journey from the vantage point of a being dynamic and ever-changing and ever-developing the power of presence and the expression of your most loving self. Each one of us expresses a part of the Divine in everything we do, and together those expressions change the world. What are we doing to create more compassion, harmony, love, and joy?

Today spend some time considering the words of inspiration and spiritual messages that help you sort through the challenges, choices, and issues you face in your own life.

Notes:

"Truly it is in the darkness that one finds the Light, then when we are in sorrow, this light is nearest to all of us." --Meister Eckart

Today we celebrate the Light of Love that shines within our hearts. Symbolically, the New Moon at its earliest degrees represents the sacrifice of the great for the good of the all, and at this point we celebrate three auspicious events that collectively represent the birth of Love within our hearts and lives.

The New Moon in its earliest degrees sits on the threshold of the Solstice gates, and unveils the path ahead. The seasons turn, the liturgical calendar brings us full circle in our celebration of life, and we honor what is holy and sacred. When we prepare to open a new door, we stand for some time at the threshold--looking back and looking forward in order to find what connects us to the whole.

Just for today, honor the sacred space between the past and the future, and be in the Presence now. Presence of the Divine, the Presence of Christ Jesus, and the Presence of all that is holy in Creation,

Just for today, celebrate the birth of Love within your own heart, and acknowledge the flow of Divine Love in and through you.

Just for today, celebrate the Light that shines within you and recognize the light in everyone and deeply infused in our experience of Life together.

Just for today, find stillness in your heart, wisdom in silence, and peace that passes all understanding, in each moment.

Just for today, let your Light shine into the darkest corners and farthest reaches of your mind.

Just for today, be filled with the Spirit of Love and Divine Light.

Inspiration:

"I will love the light for it shows me the way, yet I will endure the darkness for it shows me the stars." --Og Mandino

"It is our light not our darkness that most frightens us. We ask ourselves, who am I to be brilliant, gorgeous, talented, fabulous? Actually, who are you not to be? As we let our own light shine, we unconsciously give others permission to do the same." Marianne Williamson

"When you arise in the morning, give thanks for the morning light, for your life and your strength." Shawnee Chief, Tecumseh

"There is a light that shines beyond all things on earth, beyond the highest, the very highest heavens. This is the light that shines in your heart." Chandogya Upanishad

Biblical Citations.

Luke 2:8-11

Matthew 2:1-2

This retreat-in-daily life is about growing in intimacy with the Divine in the course of our daily lives. Sometimes our lives are fairly routine and ordinary. At other times we experience crises, major shifts and changes, or we get caught up in circumstances and conditions that cause us to feel disconnected. What we long for, is delayed. What we want to focus on gets lost to us as we are diverted by needs and events, expected and unexpected.

We have been focusing on using the background times of our days to create an interior atmosphere that allows us to wait, to hope, to come into contact with our longing and our desire.

Perhaps we can use these days to try to heighten our awareness of whatever is going on in our lives these days, and how that can bring us to whatever season in our lives we are entering. Some examples might help.

Many of us experience the ironic reality that holidays can be the most lonely time of our lives. Some of these "mixed feelings" or "sad feelings" are difficult to recognize or name.

For some of us, the holidays or special events of our lives pale in comparison to wonderful times of our past - perhaps because we were younger or more "innocent" then, perhaps because some of our loved ones who were central to our life celebrations are no longer living. Instead of looking forward to some special time, we dread it.

For some of us, we have no holy days or special events to celebrate. Some of us have no families left. How do we face the special times?

For others of us, the special times mean family conflicts. Facing the days ahead, whether they be the last few remaining parties, or conflicting demands of family and friends, or the friend or relative who drinks too much, or the experiences that we get ourselves into that takes our focus off the meaning of whatever special occasion we are celebrating. We may instead be dwelling on unrealistic expectations of ourselves or other.

What is pulling you in opposing directions? What is drawing you closer to a more authentic experience of the sacred?

Where do you feel connected to the Divine, and how does that express itself in your day to day activities? In your approach to the changes taking place in your life and in society?

What intentions are rising up in you as you continue this journey?

Each of us longs for connection and fulfillment, and each of us deals with challenges, struggles, and obstacles on our journey. When we least feel we are capable of responding or taking the next step, we often feel we have lost our way. In those moments, declare the Truth—Divine Love directs, guides, and guards us wherever we are on our journey.

Sometimes what we are being prepared for or called to do, is not obvious to us. We wonder why we have to put up with certain conditons, or what the purpose is behind all the hard work and struggles, and then, in moments of Light and illumination, we understand. We feel the purpose and connection that helps us love, serve, or support others because of what we have gone through.

When I can remain still, focus my attention and intentions on what I'm doing right now, I find it is the faith that keeps me calm and at peace. It is the faith I have, to believe that even though I cannot see a way, there is one. Even though I cannot find a solution, there is one. Even though I cannot imagine how a problem or issue can be resolved, it can and will. And that is because Divine Truth is always in the perfect place at the perfect time, working through each of us just as it is meant to. All we have to do , is keep the faith. Two women, Hannah and Miriam (Mary) depended on God to see them through troubled waters.

Scripture:

Luke 1: 46-55 The Magnificant of Mariam (Mary)

What messages are you receiving through your prayers, meditations, reflections, and the struggles in your own life?

What are you being called to do, change, or notice? What do you need on this leg of your journey?

Notes:

Today's title, "I wish to work miracles", is a quote from Leonardo da Vinci, a man who had a curiosity and passion for life like no other. One thing you may not know about Leonardo is that he died wishing he had finished more. His lust for life and desire to do more than he could do strikes a chord within each of us, I am guessing.

The holidays are times when we often feel the pressure to do more than we have time or energy for. We may have been pushing ourselves to meet deadlines, been wearing ourselves out in living up to our own expectations and those of others. We may have really enjoyed our time with family and friends, or found ourselves tested and worn out instead. Whatever your experience, let us now take some time to recuperate, rest, and restore ourselves as we prepare for the New Year.

The New Year (whichever one I am celebrating as I enjoy all the portal times of the year), is a time when I enjoy releasing, clearing, and letting go of whatever has ended, has finally been completed, or is no longer a relevant or necessary part of life. Some of the endings are painful and difficult, while others allow us to feel relieved and exhilarated. We complete certain tasks or stages of life. We lose something or someone we valued, and are left to mourn and grieve. We finally decide it is time for change, and we begin to take steps to move on or move in a new direction. For most of us, we have something to release, grieve, finish, or put aside at this time of the year.

Whenever we have the opportunity to observe these passages, we also have the gift of new sight. We can begin to see our lives with fresh eyes. We gain new perspective, and we feel energized by doing or experiencing something that we have not felt or understood before. We see on the other side of a doorway that had been closed to us before the moment when we finally were open and receptive to new insight, understanding, or awarenesses.

For now, spend some time acknowledging what you are leaving behind. Honor the passages that have taken place this year, and spend some time in quiet reflection of what you have learned or come to understand about yourself as well as about those people and experiences that matter most to you. Spend some time in contemplation of the gifts you have received from what you had the courage to let go of. Spend some time praying for support, encouragement, and guidance in whatever is still difficult to cope with.

Spend some time being receptive to your higher angels (God's thoughts) and to those supportive and loving family and friends who provide what you need in the most difficult times. Take time to express your gratitude for the gifts you have received, and cherish the time, energy, and opportunities that you have.

Consider what is most important now. How do you want to spend your time, energy, and resources, and what do you need to change in the way you are living to be able to live a life of purpose, meaning, and joy?

Inspiration:

"He judged the instant and let go; he flung himself loose into the stars."
— Annie Dillard

"Try to forgive by trying to understand how it would feel to be in the other's shoes. If someone hurts you – ask them - "What hurts you so much that you would do this?" Listen to the answer and try to understand what is valid for them. They may have been fighting for your attention, but no one thinks of themselves as attackers, only defenders! So don't judge their ways, only set them free by giving them a chance to speak. You may both learn a lot from your kindness and courage in asking for the truth. But even if nothing changes, release it, remember that you both have a right to be who you choose to be. When we make judgements we're inevitably acting on limited knowledge, so ask if you seek to understand, or simply let them be!"
— Jay Woodman

In the process of letting go you will lose many things from the past, but you will find yourself. – Deepak Chopra

When I let go of what I am, I become what I might be. When I let go of what I have, I receive what I need. – Tao Te Ching

To let go is to release the images and emotions, the grudges and fears, the clingings and disappointments of the past that bind our spirit. – Jack Kornfield

Some of us think holding on makes us strong, but sometimes it is letting go. - Herman Hesse

"I wanted a perfect ending. Now I've learned, the hard way, that some poems don't rhyme, and some stories don't have a clear beginning, middle, and end. Life is about not knowing, having to change, taking the moment and making the best of it, without knowing what's going to happen next.
Delicious Ambiguity."
— Gilda Radner

"As far as the laws of mathematics refer to reality, they are not certain; and as far as they are certain, they do not refer to reality."

— Albert Einstein

Considering the Spiritual Journey. The religious and spiritual path is a journey with constant opportunities to release, let go, and often includes forgiving. Being intentional on our journey, helps us meet the challenges and recognize the gifts of our journey. And letting go or releasing is allowing for the uncertainty of life, and having faith that we are guided, guarded, and given what we need when we need it. In other words, we are children of Grace.

Thomas a Kempis, in the spiritual classic The Imitation of Christ, advocated making a regular practice of letting go: "To sum up, dear friend of Mine, unclench your fists, and let everything fly out of your hands. Clean yourself up nicely and stay faithful to your Creator."

Biblical Citations:

Hebrews 11:1

Proverbs 17:14

I Corinthians 13:2

And if you wish to act on your desires to work miracles in your life and the lives of others, live with the full knowledge that you have all the gifts to do just that. While we cannot all do everything, we can each do something of great value, to bring great joy in our lives and the lives of those we touch. Dwell on your gifts, and allow your life to unfold with great beauty and joy.

"You crown the year with your bounty, and your carts overflow with abundance." Psalm 65:11

New Year's Eve is a moment when we stand at the threshold between the past and the future. We carry forward from this moment, what is enduring and lasting. Some of what we carry forward will help us meet new challenges and learn we are meant to learn. Some of what we carry forward will be the patterns, habits, and perspectives that we have not yet released. We carry the whole of our life with us wherever we go, yet we have the capacity to release what keeps us from growing, prospering, and enjoying the bounty of what life offers.

At this threshold today, put on the crown of your bounty. Adorn yourself with the gifts of Spirit that come in the form of hope, love, charity, and the full expression of our best selves. Take stock of what is hanging in your closet that needs to be given away--negative thinking, unhealthy habits and patterns of behavior, and worn out and lifeless remnants of what is no longer suitable for the person you have become. Wear the crown of your life's bounty as you start a new year. Move forward, over the threshold with hope, with an open heart and mind, and with a willingness to apply yourself to helping create greater peace, greater love and compassion, and greater bounty.

Bounty is the reward, the crop we harvest from the seeds and hard work we set in place in the past. Bounty is also what turns out in spite of our best efforts or lack thereof. Bounty is the fruit of our faith and trust that our energy is expressed through love, compassion, service, and the desire to share the graces that have been bestowed upon us.

Enjoy the beauty that is your life, even in the times that are difficult and hard. There is within each and every moment, something of beauty and value to be experienced. Find that something, and wear it in your crown this year. Add to the life you are living through the full expression of your highest and best self. Happy New Year.

And remember the words handed down to you as a blessing:

"A blessing for you, because the Lord your God loves you." Deuteronomy 23:5

Thoughts on the New Year.

"Hope
Smiles from the threshold of the year to come,
Whispering, 'it will be happier'..."
--Alfred Tennyson

For last year's words belong to last year's language
And next year's words await another voice.
And to make an end is to make a new beginning.

--t.s.eliot

Life is a series of natural and spontaneous changes. Don't resis them; that only creates sorrow. Let reality be reality. Let things flow naturally and forward in whatever way they like. --Lao Tzu

Some changes look negative on the surface but you will soon realize that space is being created in your life for something new to emerge. --Eckart Tolle

All that you touch, you change.
All that you change, changes you.
The only lasting truth is change.
God is change.
--Octavia Butler

"Time is not duration but intensity;
time is the beat and the interval..." --Ursula le Guin

"What can be said in New Year rhymes,
That's not been said a thousand times?
The new years come, the old years go,
We know we dream, we dream we know.
We rise up laughing with the light,
We lie down weeping with the night.
We hug the world until it stings,
We curse it then and sigh for wings.
We live, we love, we woo, we wed,
We wreathe our prides, we sheet our dead.
We laugh, we weep, we hope, we fear,
And that's the burden of a year."
--Ella Wheeler Wilcox

Biblical Inspiration.

Isaiah 43:18-19

Jeremiah 29:11

Isaiah 40:31

Proverbs 3:5-6

The lyrics to the song, River of Dreams by Billy Joel ring true as we begin the new year. The words ring true, if we allow it, every time we look at life from a new perspective.

"And in the evening,
After the fire and the light
One thing is certain;
Nothing can hold back the light
Time is relentless
And as the past disappears
We're on the verge of all things new."

Each new day, we arrive at a new threshold. We cross the threshold and all the anticipation gives way to the embracing of newness in our lives. Special times of the year and of our lives, we cross special thresholds. Daily thresholds are those liminal moments between one time and space and another when we have the opportunity to adjust our sight, become aware of our attitude, and decide how we are going to greet what is before us.

Just for today, pause between rooms when you move about the house, and spend just moments appreciating the ability you have to move freely.

Just for today, become a bit more mindful of your breath. With each inhale, allow yourself to receive with gratitude for life itself.

Just for today, look upon everything and everyone as a gift, including yourself. What gifts do you possess to share with others? What gifts have you shared of yourself?

Just for today, stop trying. Let go of the relentless need to get more done. Let yourself be enough just as you are, and honor the needs you have for rest, laughter, down time, or movement. Treat yourself to something special--an early morning run, an afternoon hike, a special cup of coffee or tea in a special cafe, a walk along the river, or a ride on your horse or bike. Stretch beyond the usual, normal, and see if every day, you can break the habitual ways of living into more creative, intentional, and enjoyable moments.

Make this day a holy day, sacred time to set the tone for how you want to live. Celebrate, share your love, express yourself in the ways that make you come alive the most, and live as if this were the most important day of your life---it is.

This is the present, the gift of presence, and all we have to do is open our eyes and hearts for the Light to come shining in to warm us up or to shed light on the corners of our being where we lack understanding. Remember it is through the cracks and broken places in our lives that the light is able to reach us. We receive our good on this day, and our lives spread out before us. Embrace each moment as you would a precious, fragile glass, and rather than worrying about breaking it, enjoy what it holds to fill you up with newness. Drink the cup of blessings for this new life we share.

Inspirational Words.

"Whatever you are physically...male or female, strong or weak, ill or healthy--all those things matter less than what your heart contains. If you have a soul of a warrior, you are a warrior. All those other things, they are the glass that contains the lamp, but you are the light inside."-- Cassandra Claire.

"Owning our story can be hard but not nearly as difficult as spending our lives running from it. Embracing our vulnerabilities is risky but not nearly as dangerous as giving up on love and belonging and joy---the experiences that make us the most vulnerable. Only when we are brave enough to explore the darkness will we discover the infinite power of our light." --Brene Brown

"How far that little candle throws his beams! So shines a good deed in a weary world." From William Shakespeare's, The Merchant of Venice

"When you get to the end of all the light you know and it's time to step into the darkness of the unknown, faith is knowing that one of two things shall happen; either you will be given something to stand on, or you will be taught how to fly." --Edward Teller (In either case, you cannot lose)

"Humankind has not woven the web of life.
We are but one thread within it.
Whatever we do to the web, we do to ourselves.
All things are bound together.
All things connect. --Chief Seattle, Duwamish, 285

Hold On

Hold on to what is good
Even if it's a handful of earth.
Hold on to what you believe
Even if it's a tree that stands by itself.
Hold on to what you must do
Even if it's a long way from here.
Hold on to your life
Even if it's easier to let go
Hold on to my hand
Even if someday I will be gone away from you.
--A Pueblo Prayer

"When you know who you are; when your mission is clear and you burn with the inner fire of unbreakable will; no cold can touch your heart, no deluge can dampen your purpose. You know that you are alive." Chief Seattle, Duwamish.

Biblical Inspiration.

Matthew 5: 13-16

The Word of God referred to the ways that God communicated with us through intuition, inner knowledge, insight, and the words of others who had received enlightenment and knowledge. Now we think of the Word as what is written, and that it can be. However, it still is what we discern through spiritual means such as dreams, discernment, intuitive knowledge, and word of knowledge that comes through others to us.

Psalms 119:105

Isaiah 60:1

From Pope Francis:

"God is the Light that illuminates the darkness, even if it does not dissolve it, and a spark of divine light is within each of us."

And also from Pope Francis:

"I believe in God - not in a Catholic God; there is no Catholic God. There is God, and I believe in Jesus Christ, his incarnation. Jesus is my teacher and my pastor, but God, the Father, Abba, is the light and the Creator. This is my Being."

In Elizabeth George's book, A Woman's Daily Walk With God, she writes,

"Your choices and decisions are a reflections of how well you have set and followed your priorities."

Living in accord with our spiritual nature and with the Greater Harmony, allows us each the freedom to live according to our higher principles, dreams, desires, and intuitive knowledge. Within each of us is a central core nature where we know ourselves as only the Divine can. Seek time today to reacquaint yourself with that central core of your own being. For when we live in accord with who we are, we have much to offer and give in all the other areas of our lives. If, however, we only live according to what we think life demands of us, or others want for us, we lose some of what makes us whole. Living in accord with your true nature is what is asked of you in this life. Listen for the sounds that strike the notes that touch your heart. Watch for the beauty that inspires your mind. Feel the essence of the Universe and all the elements, blending together to surround and comfort you on your journey, and delight in the pleasures of the gift of Life that is yours. Use it wisely, and in accord with the beating of your own heart.

Just for today, consider how do you want to spend your time and energy today? This week? This year?

Just for today, take some time to consider what really matters to you in life. What have you been putting off or delaying? What has been put on the back burner that now needs to be made an primary priority?

Just for today, consider what detracts, distracts, and drains you of energy, time, and focus.

This subject of this reflections is not about turning your back on obligations and responsibilities; rather it is about getting some perspective in how much time and energy you put into what really matters to you. Spend some time looking at your life and the way you are living it from a bit of a distance. If you would like, make a chart of your typical day and divide the chart into segments representing the time spent on each activity. Use a pie chart; it's easiest.

Notice what is missing from your life. Notice what is monopolizing most of your time and attention. The simple act of determining what you are actually doing with your time helps you gain perspective.

Next, spend some time reflecting and writing out what your main priorities are now; then make a list of what you want to change (add to your list and take away or lessen).

Many of us have lived our lives trying to do everything. We now know, either from experience or by observing the realities, that we can do much, but we cannot do everything, well. Take some time today to think about what you would like to do better this year, and what it might take in order to give yourself the gift of time, space, energy, and resources to devote yourself to what matters most to you.

Being creative, we know that our energy is activated when we are happy and doing what we love. We can feel the dynamic energy and we are able to 'leap tall buildings..." with that kind of energy. We also notice that when we are not doing what we need to be doing, we are drained, depleted, and often sick. Notice what your body, emotions, and intuition is telling you about how you are living. What needs attending to? How might you adjust your schedule, your living situation, your priorities, or your attitude?

When you do today's reflection, pay attention to your attitude and emotional responses as well as to what your are doing. Listen to the way you talk to and about yourself. What messages are you delivering with your attitude and behavior? And who and what are you living for? What and who motivates and inspires you?

A really important question to discern when setting out your priorities and making plans is your own personal code of honor. What is your code of honor? What beliefs and ideals form the parameter of your own personal code of honor? Determining what your limits, boundaries, and needs are within the framework of your own beliefs and intuitive knowledge, helps when setting forth on a new path.

Discerning priorities and setting plans accordingly, puts you more in touch with traveling the path with a sense of being authentic and living in congruence with all the guiding priorities of your life.

Just for today, determine what it is you seek and how it is you might make some small changes today to bring you more in tune with the path you are on. Avoid comparing yourself to anyone else, but instead, spend some time determining your 'bottom line'. What are your basic requirements and what do you want to accomplish, create, or do this next year?

Before making more plans, give yourself time to reflect on what matters now, and what you want to bring to fruition. After setting priorities, we establish, for ourselves, the energy that we can focus on in making new plans and in allowing the Divine to direct us towards.

Inspiration on Priorities.

The key is not to prioritize what's on your schedule, but to schedule your priorities. Stephen Covey

Do not postpone what's important to you simply because others don't share your priorities." Hemal Jhaveri

Every human has four endowments - self awareness, conscience, independent will and creative imagination. These give us the ultimate human freedom... The power to choose, to respond, to change.

A simple life is not seeing how little we can get by with--that's poverty--but how efficiently we can put first things first...When you're clear about your purpose and priorities, you can painlessly discard whatever does not support these, whether it's clutter in your cabinets or commitments on your calendar." --Victoria Moran, Lit from Within: Tending Your Soul for Lifelong Beauty

" A man [we] should not strive to eliminate our complexities but to get into accord with them; they are legitimately what directs our conduct in the world." Freud

"Action expresses priorities." Mahatma Ghandi

"Most of us spend too much time on what is urgent and not enough time on what is important." Stephen Covey

"Things which matter most must never be at the mercy of things which matter least." Goethe

"Every hour you are not going after your passion, making your dreams a reality or defining your purpose is an hour you can't get back. Is what you're doing right now, this day, this moment getting you closer to where you want to be? If not, readjust your focus. It's your future. Go get it!"

--Elizabeth Bougeret

"The first day of the brand new calendar year is an empowered time to psychologically unwind to mentally find own life charged emotionally with a refined energy & enthusiasm to create a beautiful growth paradigm within the physically defined laws of nature and the rules of the game called life."

Biblical Passages on Priorities.

Phillipians 4: 6-8

Ecclesiastes 3:13, NLT ...people should eat and drink and enjoy the fruits of their labor, for these are gifts from God.

Luke 12:34

Romans 12:2,

Proverbs 24:27,

Enjoy spinning dreams, weaving tapestries of longing, and spending time honoring that within you that longs to be born.

"The way of the Creative works through change and transformation, so that each thing receives its true nature and destiny and comes into permanent accord with the Great Harmony; this is what furthers and what perseveres." --Alexander Pope

27/40 Taproot: Finding Our Home

In a plant, the taproot is the primary root that grows downward into the ground, and out of which all other, smaller roots are formed. When used to describe our lives, the taproot is that essence of our being that is the principal source of growth and development. Regardless of our age or stage of life, we each continue to be affected by our connections to the taproot of our own being.

At times we remain unconscious of the vital connection. At such times, we may feel disconnected, dissatisfied, or depressed for we are cut off from our life source. When we lose sight of what makes us feel alive and authentic, it is because we have lost sight of what really matters.

Why does this happen? It happens when we get so wrapped up in finding ourselves through a relationship to another person, a job, an idea or cause that we forget our essential nature and essence.

Just for today, take some time to contemplate all the ways you feel connected to your essence. What family ties and geographic locations speak to you of home? What makes you feel at home, safe, and secure? What about you and your life has lasting value and what holds meaning for you?

When asked this question by a group of young middle-schoolers many years ago, I answered, "Ask yourself what it is that you would never want to be without in your life. What would you love to do everyday, regardless of what else was happening? What are you passionate about, and how would you like to use this passion? It is that thing, that purpose that will drive you regardless of what you study, where you travel, what you do with your life, or who is in it. Find that essence, that passion, and the road will open up for you to live a purposeful and fulfilling life."

I believe this question is relevant at any time or age. It's a question I ask myself in those times when I'm feeling cut off or uninspired. It is a question that I ask to keep me in touch with what really matters in life. It is a question worth asking. Then listen and watch for the answers that rise up along your path today. When we need to rediscover connection, start with that which brings you life.

For many years, I taught language and culture to people from all over the world. One of the things we all had in common was our desire to learn and use the language. Language is home for many of us. It is how we communicate about everything. It is how we come to understand ourselves, to name and describe who we are and what holds meaning. Language for so many is one of the only places where they feel at home in strange and unfamiliar places.

We each respond to different languages. There are the languages of our homelands, our Mother tongue. There are the languages of the fields we are passionate about—the language of the sciences, the languages of technology, the languages of art, and the languages of music. Language, our desire to communicate and be understood, is one of the deepest aspects of our being. Just for today, consider which languages root you and connect you to home within.

Just for today, ask yourself, "What brings me life?"

Just for today, allow yourself quiet, reflective time to simply ask a question (subconsciously or aloud in prayer), and wait for an answer. Sometimes we experience prayer as a non-stop verbal expression from ourselves to the Divine—begging, thanking, lamenting, questioning, praising, struggling with, or seeking answers and solutions.

Just for today, let your prayer be about listening and watching to how the Divine is filling your life with answers to your questions.

Just for today, look deep into how you are connected. Notice where you feel disconnected—those relationships that haven't worked out or that don't fulfill your expectations. Notice the difference between what you long for and what you already have.

Just for today, notice where you are rooted, and consider how your experiences, connections, losses, and gifts have contributed to your present essence. Who and what in your life give you the nourishment, sense of connection, and meaning you need (relationships, animals, nature, the elements, music, dance, art, literature, adventure, discovery)?

Just for today, consider what is essential for your well being and happiness. And nurture that with your love and attention.

Just for today, think of what and who has nurtured and helped you grow and develop, and put your attention and love into sharing that with others. How can your experiences (successes and losses) help you support and nurture others?

Inspiration:

"All that is gold does not glitter,
Not all those who wander are lost;
The old that is strong does not wither,
Deep roots are not reached by the frost.

From the ashes a fire shall be woken,
A light from the shadows shall spring;
Renewed shall be blade that was broken,
The crownless again shall be king."
— J.R.R. Tolkien, The Fellowship of the Ring

"For me, trees have always been the most penetrating preachers. I revere them when they live in tribes and families, in forests and groves. And even more I revere them when they stand alone... Trees are sanctuaries. Whoever knows how to speak to them, whoever knows how to listen to them, can learn the truth. They do not preach learning and precepts, they preach, undeterred by particulars, the ancient law of life.

A tree says: A kernel is hidden in me, a spark, a thought, I am life from eternal life. The attempt and the risk that the eternal mother took with me is unique, unique the form and veins of my skin, unique the smallest play of leaves in my branches and the smallest scar on my bark. I was made to form and reveal the eternal in my smallest special detail." -Herman Hesse

"Maybe your country is only a place you make up in your own mind. Something you dream about and sing about. Maybe it's not a place on the map at all, but just a story full of people you meet and places you visit, full of books and films you've been to. I'm not afraid of being homesick and having no language to live in. I don't have to be like anyone else. I'm walking on the wall and nobody can stop me."
— Hugo Hamilton, The Speckled People: A Memoir of a Half-Irish Childhood

"Language is the only homeland."
— Czesław Miłosz

"I'm planting a tree to teach me to gather strength from my deepest roots." — Andrea Koehle Jones, The Wish Trees

"Focus on faith and grow your roots strong and deep so no one can make you believe in something that is not good for your soul."
— Molly Friedenfeld

"Some say that my teaching is nonsense.

Other call it lofty but impractical.
But to those who have looked inside themselves,
this nonsense makes perfect sense.
And to those who put it into practice,
this loftiness has roots that go deep."
— Lao Tzu, Tao Te Ching

"If we are the trees, words are our roots; and we grow as we write"
— Munia Khan

"Leaving home's a cinch. It's the staying, once you've found it, that takes courage."
— Catherine Watson

"The pull of the mountain is like gravity for my soul."
— Heather Day Gilbert, Miranda Warning

Consider a tree for a moment. As beautiful as trees are to look at, we don't see what goes on underground - as they grow roots. Trees must develop deep roots in order to grow strong and produce their beauty. But we don't see the roots. We just see and enjoy the beauty. In much the same way, what goes on inside of us is like the roots of a tree. —Joyce Meyer

All things must come to the soul from its roots, from where it is planted. —Saint Teresa of Avila

Biblical Citations:

Daniel 415 NIV

Hosea 14:5

Colassians 2:7 NIV

Jeremiah 17:8

Ezekiel 17:7

Isaiah 32:18

Proverbs 24:3-4

One of the most powerful and beautiful stories in the Hebrew Biblical Scriptures/Old Testament, is the story of Ruth and Naomi. It speaks to us of so many layers of our lives, of love and loss, of home and alienation, and of friendship and devotion. Find a piece of yourself in their tale.

Read the story of Ruth, Ruth 1:6-18, and then consider the following:

What part of this story can you identify with? What must it have been like to be part of this story? How does this speak to your own life, and the struggles, situations, and supportive relationships you have?

Notes:

Mark Twain once remarked, "I can teach anybody how to get what they want out of life. The problem is that I can't find anybody who can tell me what they want."

When we seek to deepen our spiritual journey, we often rely on sources outside ourselves. This is one way we seek meaning and purpose, and it is a noble way to pursue spiritual knowledge. Reading the works of spiritual masters, spending time with those whose wisdom is greater than our own, or looking for meaning through service, devotion, praise, and spiritual and religious traditions. All are part of how we seek knowledge and how we discover and understand what life is about.

One thing we often hesitate to do is to look within. Today I suggest we do a little spiritual mining. The idea is not mine but that of author, Marcel Proust. In the late 1800s while a teenager, long before Proust had become known as one of the greatest authors of all time, he filled out a questionnaire give to him by his friend, Antoinette. She was the daughter of the French President. In Victorian times, young women kept a confession album--the Victorian version of contemporary personality tests. A young woman would give the questionnaire to a friend in order to learn more about their true personality. It was not until 1924, two years after his death, that this form was found and made public.

Since then, the questionnaire has been used by interviewers to interview guests on their shows or for their publications. The questions provide an excellent way for asking yourself what really matters to you---what is essential in your life? It also helps us express what it is that we believe. We talk a lot about our beliefs and opinions, but how often do we actually try to explore just what those beliefs are?

Today I invite you to use these questions to explore what is essential for you. Add your own questions, change the ones presented here to fit your own needs, and periodically, use the questionnaire to stay in touch with who you are, how you change, and what remains steady within you, as well as what is fluid and growing. Enjoy the process, and write out your answers in your journal or meditate on the questions themselves, and see what rises us for you. Here's to what is essential.

Questionnaire:

What is your idea of perfect happiness?

What do you consider your greatest accomplishment?

What is your greatest fear?

What historical figure do you most identify with?

What living person do you most admire? Why?

Who are your heroes and heroines in real life?

What is the trait you most deplore in yourself?

What is the trait you most deplore in others?

What is your favorite journey?

What do you consider the most overrated virtue?

Which words and phrases do you most overuse?

What is your greatest regret?

What is your current state of mind?

If you could change one thing about your family, what would it be?

What is your most treasured possession?

Where would you like to live?

What's your favorite way to spend time?

What quality do you like most in a woman? In a man?

What quality do you like most about yourself?

What are your favorite names?

What is your motto?

What is your theme song?

Questions I would add:

Who/What is God/the Divine to you?

How does your conception of the Holy affect the way you live your life?

What would you like to release from your life?

What would you like to change or add to your life?

Do you believe that people and life is basically good or basically bad?

What do you believe is possible to change or improve about yourself or your life?

Where do you feel connected? Where do you feel disconnected?

Enjoy the process of asking yourself these questions, and allow yourself to listen to your answers. Pull these questions out periodically, and see how your perspective, feelings, and attitudes change over time.

Words of Inspiration:

"Like an old gold-panning prospector, you must resign yourself to digging up a lot of sand from which you will later patiently wash out a few minute particles of gold ore." --Dorothy Bryant.

"I think somehow we learn who we really are and then we live with that decision." --Eleanor Roosevelt.

"People go abroad to wonder at the heights of mountains, at the huge waves of the sea, at the long courses of the rivers, at the vast compass of the ocean, at the circular motions of the stars, and they pass by themselves without wondering." St. Augustine.

"One must know oneself. If this does not serve to discover truth, it at least serves as a rule of life and there is nothing better." -- Blaise Pascal

"One's own self is well hidden from one's own self; of all mines of treasure, one's own is the last to be dug up." Friedrich Wilhelm Nietzsche

"The only journey is the journey within." – Rainer Maria Rilke.

Biblical Passages:

Psalms 77: 6

Psalms 139: 14-16

Lamentations 3:40

I Corinthians 11:28

Romans 12:2

Romans 12: 6-7

Matthew 5: 5-10

1 Timothy 4:4

Delight in your Divine Beauty, rejoice and be glad for all the Gifts of Spirit that fill you and unfold in your life.

"The white light streams down to be broken up by those human prisms into all the colors of the rainbow. Take your own color in the pattern and be just that." Charles Brown.

When asked what the greatest commandment was, Jesus answered by saying, " Love the Lord your God with all your heart and with all your soul, and with all your mind. The second is like it. "Love your neighbor as yourself." When we look at how we humans treat one another, we might have some idea of why there is so much strife in the world. Loving ourselves is essential to loving others, to living out our spiritual purpose, and to expressing our love of the Divine. Sometimes we mistake egotism for self love; at other times we berate ourselves in thought, word, and deed, undervaluing and denigrating our essential goodness.

What is essential for having a healthy sense of self love? How can we be more loving to ourselves and others?

Begin by listening to how you talk to and about yourself. How often do honor your essence, your goodness, and your gifts? How often do you sell yourself short, criticize and complain about yourself and your life, or plant negative seeds and doubts in your own thinking? Just for today, listen to how you talk to yourself, and begin changing the tone of your inner communication, from negative and fear-based talk to uplifting and affirming language. How we talk and think about ourselves determines how we feel about ourselves. It also colors the way we understand and view others.

Begin affirming who you are with prayers and mantras that instill truth and Divine Love within you. Just for today, find a mantra or phrase that is uplifting and repeat it over and over to yourself, in quiet moments when you are alone, while driving or waiting in line, or when doing a task like washing the dishes or cleaning off your desk. Our mind, heart, and soul respond to words of love, and we need to remind ourselves that "God is Love, and I am a reflection of that Love", "God loves and accepts me as I am, and so do I", or "Divine Love protects, Divine Intelligence directs, Divine Mind unfolds each day, all we should know, or do, or say." Find a mantra, scripture, or prayer that works for you, and water your soul's garden with messages of love today.

Just for today, take good care of yourself by nourishing your inner being in healthy ways. Just for today, treat yourself with the utmost respect and care. Eat with intention and select foods and beverages as you would in preparation for a great feast or gala celebration. Honor the gifts of Life that are provided for you, and live today with great regard for yourself as a gift of the Great Creator, lovingly made.

One of my favorite verses from Psalms speaks of how unique and special each person is. When we can recognize this in ourselves, it makes it more likely we will recognize this in others. Psalms 139:

"For you created my inmost being; you knit me together in my Mother's

womb."

Just for today, remember to love that precious child within you that was

loved, adored, and welcomed into this life to live and give glory to God.

Words of Inspiration..

" He who travels in search of something which he has not got, travels

away from himself and grows old even in youth among old things."

--Ralph Waldo Emerson

"Every time you do not follow your inner guidance, you feel a loss of

energy, loss of power, a sense of spiritual deadness." --Shakti Gawain

"Be who you are and say what you feel, because those who mind don't

matter and those who matter won't mind." --Dr. Seuss

"You will always find those who think they know what is your duty better than you know it."
Ralph Waldo Emerson

All my life I had been looking for something, and everywhere I turned someone tried to tell me
what it was. I accepted their answers too, though they were often in contradiction and even self
contradictory. I was naive. I was looking for myself and asking everyone except myself
questions which I, and only I, could answer. It took me a long time and much painful
boomeranging of my expectations to achieve a realization everyone else appears to have been
born with; that I am nobody but myself." -- Ralph Ellison

[And of course, most of us are not born with this awareness; we make the same types of forays
onto paths that others have taken. Finding our own path requires that we honor our own truths
and our right and obligation to be ourselves.)

"You must have control of the authorship of your own destiny. The pen that writes your life story must be held in your own hand."
--Irene C. Kassorla

"Almost every man[person] wastes part of life in attempts to display
qualities which he does not possess, and to gain applause which he cannot keep." Samuel Johnson, 1750

"There is just one life for each of us; our own." --Euripedes

"The most exhausting thing in life is being insincere." Anne Morrow Lindbergh

"Be open. And the the truth follows." --Gamgaji

"Like the sky opens after a rainy day, we must open to ourselves...Learn to love yourself for who you are and open so the world can see you shine." James Poland

"All the knowledge I possess everyone else can acquire, but my heart is all my own." Johnann von Goethe.

Biblical Quotes.

1 Samuel 16:7

Psalms 139: 14-16

Romans 12: 2

Romans 12: 6-7

Proverbs 6:3

Proverbs 23

1 Timothy 4:4

Jerimiah 29:11

Matthew 12:37

"Muddy water, let stand, becomes clear."
— Lao Tzu

Curiosita, is "an insatiably curious approach to life and an unrelenting quest for continuous learning." It is one of the seven principles illustrated by the life of the great artist, scientist, inventor, and thinker, Leonardo da Vinci. Curiosita is an the part of our character which seeks to explore, discover, and open up to the mysteries, hidden treasures, and boundlessness of our own souls. Leonardo da Vinci once said, "The desire to know is natural."

Living life in the contemporary world, we find ourselves caught up in a whirlwind of activities, obligations, and tasks. Much of our day is spent engaged in one activity after another. Even as we wake, our minds fill with lists of activities, chores, or ideas that we feel need attending to. "Where will I stay on my trip?". "Will I have time to eat before my first session?" "Wonder where I left that paper I need to fill out?" Our mind is filled with little pieces of thought--thoughts that tie us up in the future or trap us in the past. Even when we are engaged in a conversation, our minds might be wandering, carrying us out of the presence of the person we are with. We joke about someone else's short attention span, yet our own is often like that of a gnat. Better we should emulate the bee.

Bees are a study in concentration. When a bee is engaged in sipping nectar from a flower, it hovers in perfect attention, its little bee body completely engaged in the process of attaining its goal. Bees have two stomachs; one for processing food, the other for storing nectar and water to be taken back to the hive and used to make honey. Picking up pollen on its feet, it then moves flits from flower to flower, taking pollen from one flower to another--a kind of accidental benefit. Bees do not intentionally pollenate plants, but do so as a result of their search for nectar to make honey. Back in the beehive, the worker bees store the nectar and water which forms honey. They store this in the beeswax along with their babies.

What does the bee have to do with concentration and contemplation? When was the last time you stopped the mad dash of life to simply contemplate the simple acts or behavior of an insect like a bee or butterfly? When was the last time you sat quietly observing someone's movement or another person's features? When was the last time you sat before the ocean and observed its changes and different characteristics? Bees are important to the subject as an example of how our attention can fix itself on something beyond our own concerns and preoccupations. Curiosita is that element of our being that seeks to grow beyond the limitations and self-imposed boundaries that trap us in routine, lifeless tasks, or unimaginative lifestyles.

Just for today, spend some time in quiet contemplation of the simple gifts of life that surround you. Watch your animals, and hone in on the energy that is created in and around them when you take time to simply observe them being themselves. Listen to the sounds of the world around you--the ship's whistle blowing out warnings through the fog on the river. The hum of traffic on the highway up the hill, the sounds of the glass table jiggling as one of the cats jumps up to perch on it and to watch the morning flight of the birds outside the window. The quaking of the ducks, sounds within your own body, the humming of the appliances. Use your eyes and powers of concentration to observe the life unfolding right before your eyes. Take out a drawing tablet and a pencil and sketch the scene right in front of you. Let your drawing be what it is, and avoid worrying about 'how good the drawing is'...simply capture some of what you see and feel in this moment.

Contemplation is a tool of Curiosita, and is a treasure that can unlock your imagination. Concentration and contemplation can assist you in honing your powers of observation and help perfect your ability to listen and really hear. As a teacher, I found it important to rein in my need to fill in silences when a question had been posed. Instead, I let silence work as a sacred place for people to dig into their own minds, hearts, and centers to dig up something of value to pull out and express. Silence works beautifully for allowing the imagination, intuition, spirit, and mind to work their way to the surface to be expressed in some way.

Allow yourself some time to wholly focus on something or someone, and get out of the way to allow that object, idea, or person to light up before your eyes. Use your journal or your sketch pad to capture bits of what is appearing to you. Capture the essence of the idea that is presenting itself to you, and then sit in silence a while longer letting yourself be fully present with that which is before you, within you, or somewhere in the landscape of your own life.

One of my greatest joys and a source of deep contemplative thought are other peoples' gardens. While out walking, I love to take in the beauty that others have worked so hard to create around them. The fragrances, colors, patterns, hidden treasures, and both organized and neatly arranged gardens and chaotic, profuse, and overgrown gardens bring great delight on a contemplative walk. The overgrown berry branches that grow up through the railroad trestles, or the fragrant sage or fig trees on the side of an island hillside, all become part of my collection of images, imagination, and memories, the tools for writing, painting, and creating stories to explain some small piece of the profound beauty of life.

Words of Inspiration.:

Faith and reason are like two wings on which the human spirit rises to the contemplation of truth ; and God has placed in the human heart a desire to know the truth in a word, to know himself so that, by knowing and loving God, men and women may also come to the fullness of truth about themselves. Pope John Paul II

A rose plant has leaves, thorns and flowers. Concentration helps you to identify as to where the thorns are and the flower is. To cut the love (rose flower) away from worldly desires (thorns) is contemplation. Concentration is identifying the various locations of the thorns and flowers by looking at the rose plant. To offer the flower, so cut, to the Lord is meditation.

From the diaries of Victor Frankl while in the concentration camps:

"This intensification of inner life helped the prisoner find a refuge from the emptiness, desolation and spiritual poverty of his existence, by letting him escape into the past. When given free rein, his imagination played with past events, often not important ones, but minor happenings and trifling things. His nostalgic memory glorified them and they assumed a strange character. Their world and their existence seemed very distant and the spirit reached out for them longingly: In my mind I took bus rides, unlocked the front door of my apartment, answered my telephone, switched on the electric lights. Our thoughts often centered on such details, and these memories could move one to tears.

"As the inner life of the prisoner tended to become more intense, he also experienced the beauty of art and nature as never before. Under their influence he sometimes even forgot his own frightful circumstances. If someone had seen our faces on the journey from Auschwitz to a Bavarian camp as we beheld the mountains of Salzburg with their summits glowing in the sunset, through the little barred windows of the prison carriage, he would never have believed that those were the faces of men who had given up all hope of life and liberty. Despite that factor--or maybe because of it--we were carried away by nature's beauty, which we had missed for so long.

"A garden to walk in and immensity to dream in--what more could he ask? A few flowers at his feet and above him the stars."
— Victor Hugo, Les Misérables

"When I look out on such a night as this, I feel as if there could be neither wickedness nor sorrow in the world; and there certainly would be less of both if the sublimity of Nature were more attended to, and people were carried more out of themselves by contemplating such a scene."
— Jane Austen

"If there were a little more silence, if we all kept quiet...maybe we could understand something."
— Federico Fellini

"Usually, when the distractions of daily life deplete our energy, the first thing we eliminate is the thing we eliminate is the thing we need the most: quiet, reflective time. Time to dream, time to contemplate what's working and what's not, so that we can make changes for the better. (January 17)"

— Sarah Ban Breathnach, Simple Abundance: A Daybook of Comfort and Joy

"Seeking the face of God in everything, everyone, all the time, and his hand in every happening; This is what it means to be contemplative in the heart of the world. Seeing and adoring the presence of Jesus, especially in the lowly appearance of bread, and in the distressing disguise of the poor."
— Mother Teresa, In the Heart of the World: Thoughts, Stories and Prayers

"Life is an experimental journey undertaken involuntarily. It is a journey of the spirit through the material world and, since it is the spirit that travels, it is the spirit that is experienced. That is why there exist contemplative souls who have lived more intensely, more widely, more tumultuously than others who have lived their lives purely externally."

— Fernando Pessoa, The Book of Disquiet

"How happy we would be if we could find the treasure of which the Gospel speaks; all else would be as nothing. As it is boundless, the more you search for it the greater the riches you will find; let us search unceasingly and let us not stop until we have found it."
— Brother Lawrence, The Practice of the Presence of God

"What we plant in the soil of contemplation, we will reap in the harvest of action." Meister Eckart

Biblical Quotes.

Psalms 46:10

Psalms 107: 43 ."

Psalms 111:2

Notes:

"By seeking and blundering we learn."
— Johann Wolfgang von Goethe

Dimostrazione, is a concept that means one's commitment to test knowledge through experience, persistence, and a willingness to learn from mistakes. When we use our beliefs preconceptions, assumptions, and past experiences to become a wall that blocks us from understanding or seeing what needs to change in our lives, we prevent our own growth and development. My Mother used to warn me about 'resting on my laurels'---being content to the point of apathy with what I had already accomplished or learned.

The dynamism that directs our lives is constantly turning over new soil, bringing us new challenges and lessons to learn, and calling us to be more aware. Today our challenge is to consider some of our own basic assumptions and normal patterns of thinking and behavior.

Just for today, consider how you may be deceived by your own opinions. Which of your beliefs and opinions are truly your own? Take some time to think about how the concept of dimostrazione works in your own life. What beliefs of yours have you challenged, and what happened when you did that? When was the last time you made a major change in the way you believe, the way you behave, or the way you understand and look at life?

Just for today, ponder what sources you rely on to determine your beliefs and opinions. How original and independent is your thinking? Think of when you learned something, and what that felt like. Think of when you struggled and maybe failed to learn something or do something that was important to you. Consider how you have learned from your mistakes, and how your thinking, perceptions, opinions, or attitudes have changed as a result of some major lesson in life.

We learn through our failures and mistakes as much as we learn through our successes and accomplishments. Just for today, consider some of the most important or most difficult areas of your life, and thing about how you can view the experience from different perspectives.

When Leonardo da Vinci wanted to test himself and question his experiences and failures (and yes, he had many failures in his life), he would attempt to view a situation, problem, or question from three different angles. See if you can view one of your opinions or beliefs from three different perspectives--from a distance, from an opposite or reverse point-of-view, or from the viewpoint of someone younger, older, or of the opposite gender. Choose the viewpoints from which to view your choice.

Try to determine which of your opinions or beliefs are based on 'false advertising'--something you have been convinced of even though it may not be true. Sometimes our beliefs or opinions are as they are because we have never questioned them at all; at other times they are as they are because we have accepted something as fact that is not.

For today, explore your attitudes about making mistakes. Ask yourself, "What would I do/have done differently, if I could?" You might also try to identify the feelings you get when you feel you have made a mistake or failed at something. What do those feelings tell you about some underlying fear or sense of shame? Where does that come from?

Spend some time today, examining your own feelings and beliefs about relationships, your own spirituality and religious ideas, money and finances, learning, creating, and living out your life purpose.

As you spend some time today exploring your own journey, complete with mistakes, obstacles, setbacks, failures, and dead-ends, notice what opinions, beliefs, and understanding tend to rule your thinking and behavior when you are under stress or suffering some kind of personal defeat or loss. We tend to feel a lot of shame for falling down, and even though we all do struggle, have difficult challenges, and meet with defeat, we seldom talk about it, hoping instead to 'do better next time', or 'try, try again', or 'learn from our mistakes'.

Much like anything in life, if we are not willing to acknowledge what needs attention, it's very unlikely we can learn not to make the same mistakes again. Have courage and charge forward, exploring those areas of your life and belief system (including opinions, fantasies, and hopes), and see what they have to tell you about where you might be willing to learn and change to bring more peace, joy, fulfillment, and self-acceptance into your life.

Words of Inspiration..

"We are products of our past, but we don't have to be prisoners of it."
— Rick Warren, The Purpose Driven Life: What on Earth Am I Here for?

"Many times what we perceive as an error or failure is actually a gift. And eventually we find that lessons learned from that discouraging experience prove to be of great worth."
— Richelle E. Goodrich, Smile Anyway: Quotes, Verse, & Grumblings for Every Day of the Year

"You will only fail to learn if you do not learn from failing."
— Stella Adler, The Art of Acting

"We do not learn from experience... we learn from reflecting on experience." --John Dewey

"Sometimes…
Sometimes doubt is the opposite of faith, but sometimes doubt can be a pathway to faith.
Sometimes weakness is the opposite of strength, but sometimes weakness can be the pathway to strength.
Sometimes addiction is the opposite of sobriety, but sometimes addiction can be the pathway to sobriety.
Sometimes infidelity is the opposite of fidelity, but sometimes infidelity can be a pathway to fidelity.

Sometimes failure is the opposite of success, but sometimes failure can be the pathway to success."
— David W. Jones

Our greatest mistakes, if we look at them, and digest them, and interact with them, and learn from them… they can be the greatest moments of our lives."
— Dan Pearce

"In religion and politics people's beliefs and convictions are in almost every case gotten at second-hand, and without examination, from authorities who have not themselves examined the questions at issue but have taken them at second-hand from other non-examiners, whose opinions about them were not worth a brass farthing."
— Mark Twain

"All religions lead to the same God, and all deserve the same respect. Anyone who chooses a religion is also choosing a collective way for worshipping and sharing the mysteries. Nevertheless, that person is the only one responsible for his or her actions along the way and has no right to shift responsibility for any personal decisions on to that religion."
— Paulo Coelho

"Alice laughed. 'There's no use trying,' she said. 'One can't believe impossible things.'

I daresay you haven't had much practice,' said the Queen. 'When I was your age, I always did it for half-an-hour a day. Why, sometimes I've believed as many as six impossible things before breakfast. There goes the shawl again!"
— Lewis Carroll

"If you don't change your beliefs, your life will be like this forever. Is that good news?"
— W. Somerset Maugham

And in the final analysis, your beliefs and opinions are your own. What you choose to do with them, is your business. As we go through this part of our retreat-in-daily life, it is up to each of us to determine what is most essential for our personal growth, happiness, development, and spiritual journey. What at this time in your life, is worthy of examining? What inner truth is worthy of the effort and courage needed to face your own truth? And what is worthy of changing so you can move into a deeper experience of life?

Biblical Quotes.

Ecclesiastes 4:11

Proverbs 9:9

Proverbs 1:1-33

1 John 4:18

Hebrews 4:12

Isaiah 41:10

Notes:

"Slow down, and everything that you are chasing will
come around and catch you." --John Da Paola

Recently in a meditation group, someone mentioned the struggle in dealing with life's ambiguities. Sfumato, which literally means, 'up in smoke' or "turned to mist" is a term that connotes a willingness to embrace the ambiguity, paradox, and uncertainty that characterizes much of our life experiences. Sfumato is a term used by artists to describe the hazy, mysterious qualities of artists like Leonardo da Vinci. This mysterious, hazy quality is something that colors our own lives as well.

The more deeply we look into the experience of living the lives we live, the more our senses are awakened and the more we understand that there are no simple, cut-and-dried answers or solutions to many things. Uncertainty and the dynamism of life assures us that just when we get comfortable, changes will occur, events will happen, or we will be drawn to learn and grow in a new way. Our physical lives are full of polarities, some of which we fight and others which we seem to be able to integrate into a harmonious balance. This tension of opposites, is something alive within each of us. And throughout our lives our challenge is often on how to bring that tension in balance.

Today, let's play with some of the concepts that we experience, by using another means of expressing what ambiguity, uncertainty, and paradox might be like for us. Sometimes when we explore ideas, feelings, emotions, or ambiguous and paradoxical experiences, we are at a loss of words to explain or understand. Just for today, use other means of exploring your idea, feelings, emotions, or relationships (to yourself, to others, to your work, to your art, to any of the important aspects of your life). Draw or paint what ambiguity looks like. Dance paradox, Sing about uncertainty. Explore a relationship through the use of some physical activity or creation. Create a mobile or totem to Ambiguity, paradox, or uncertainty.

Using our senses and exploring our thoughts, feelings, emotions, and senses through media other than language (written or spoken), often opens us up to understanding the whole of what the polarities in our lives are like for us. Day to day, we deal with choices, options, and different perspectives. Today, let us explore these seemingly conflicting elements of our being in ways that allow us to find a portion of what is need to cope with the conflicts in your life.

Next, contemplate some of the ways that you cultivate endurance of confusion. How do you deal with joy and sorrow? What are the struggles you have with intimacy versus your need for independence? How do you deal with your strengths and weaknesses? How do you define good and evil, and how do you cope with it in your own experience? What battles do you wage between your need for change and that of consistency? How are you engaging in the experiences of humility and pride? How have you learned to handle the conflict between goals versus process? How do life and death inform your experience of living and being a spiritual being?

Make space in your life today. Give yourself a little more time and room to be. Take one minute to simply gaze at something or someone. Allow yourself to have an extra minute walking towards a destination. Slow down a bit, and move more slowly into a busy, hectic situation. Walk away from a situation or problem that needs handling--give yourself some space and time away from the situation and watch what happens. Often great ideas come when taking a shower or while on a walk. Walk away from a situation you find perplexing, and allow some time. See what happens.

Spend more time doing a simple task. Take longer than you usually do to do something like washing dishes, feeding your animals, taking out the recycling, or straightening up your desk.

Wait before responding. Slow down your response time. I learned while working a high-powered job, that not everything is equally important, and most things did not require my immediate attention. Actually, I learned this earlier, but the busier I get, the more apparent it becomes. The power went out last week for several hours, and I was unable to work at my usual clip. Instead, I had to take time, wait, and do everything more slowly. Rather than waiting for the power to go out, slow yourself down. Allow your breathing to deepen, and let yourself feel less pressured to be, do, respond, or fix things immediately. Take it easy for a change. And for those who are saying, "I don't have time to do that" I say, you don't have time not to do this. Your productivity will increase, the stress in your life and its effects on your body will lessen, and you will enjoy and be more present for whatever it is you are doing.

And during these little bits of time and space, be open, with all your senses and with your intuitive essence, to be aware of where you are connected to that which enlivens you, that which infuses you with the Divine spark of life, and notice how and where you feel guided, led, or shown something you might have missed had you not taken just a little more time.

Get used to waiting, and allowing yourself to be fully present in the waiting spaces. Notice how being more at home with, embracing the in-between times, opens you to possibilities, the next step, or an answer you may have been seeking.

Hesitate before responding, adding your 'two cents' or giving your opinion. Just allow whatever you are hearing or observing to act to be what it is--without your interference or help. Let yourself be free of the overwhelming urge or sense of obligation, to fix, solve, or have your say about everything.

It will be interesting to see how this works. Our cultural environment has us on constant 'high alert' to be attentive, to be busy, and to get the next thing done even before we have finished what we are doing. Being able to let go of the need to react, respond, or be active all the time, allows for a greater understanding of what is essential to being present and aware of the life we are living now.

Words of Inspiration..

"To learn which questions are unanswerable, and not to answer them: this skill is most needful in times of stress and darkness."   Ursula Le Guin

"The awareness of the ambiguity of one's highest achievements - as well as one's deepest failures - is a definite symptom of maturity."
— Paul Tillich

As human beings, not only do we seek resolution, but we also feel that we deserve resolution. However, not only do we not deserve resolution, we suffer from resolution. We don't deserve resolution; we deserve something better than that. We deserve our birthright, which is the middle way, an open state of mind that can relax with paradox and ambiguity."
— Pema Chödrön, When Things Fall Apart: Heart Advice for Difficult Times

"Running through the maze of life, you come across profound ambiguities and complexities. Yet the essence of living a meaningful life, remains simple--following your heart and pursuing your life purpose."— Roopleen

"Nobody knows what will happen after five minutes later! Strangely, this ambiguity makes life very interesting!"
— Mehmet Murat ildan

"Everything you've learned in school as "obvious" becomes less and less obvious as you begin to study the universe. For example, there are no solids in the universe. There's not even a suggestion of a solid. There are no absolute continuums. There are no surfaces. There are no straight lines."
— Buckminster Fuller

"In order to be open to creativity, one must have the capacity for contructive use of solitude. One must overcome the fear of being alone." --Rollo May

"Il n'est pas certain que tout soit incertain.
(Translation: It is not certain that everything is uncertain.)"
— Blaise Pascal, Pascal's Pensees

"It's the side-by-side culture of the Talmud I like so much. 'On the one hand' and 'on the other hand' is frustrating for people seeking absolute faith, but for me it gives religion an ambidextrous quality that suits my temperament."
— Jonathan Rosen, The Talmud and the Internet: A Journey between Worlds

"As far as the laws of mathematics refer to reality, they are not certain; and as far as they are certain, they do not refer to reality."
— Albert Einstein

"When in doubt, be ridiculous."
— Sherwood Smith, Firebirds: An Anthology of Original Fantasy

Ali Edwards, author and designer says, "Do nothing. I have a habit of welcoming time away from my creative work. For me this is serious life-recharging time where my only responsibility is to just be Mom & Wife & Me. Doing nothing has a way of synthesizing what is really important in my life and in my work and inspires me beyond measure. When I come back to work I am better equipped to weed out the non-essential stuff and focus on the things I most want to express creatively.

"When I am, as it were, completely myself, entirely alone, and of good cheer–say, traveling in a carriage or walking after a good meal or during the night when I cannot sleep–it is on such occasions that my ideas flow best and most abundantly." --Amadeus Mozart

Albert Einstein remarked, "Although I have a regular work schedule, I take time to go for long walks on the beach so that I can listen to what is going on inside my head. If my work isn't going well, I lie down in the middle of a workday and gaze at the ceiling while I listen and visualize what goes on in my imagination."

Kafka: "You need not leave your room. Remain sitting at your table and listen. You need not even listen, simply wait, just learn to become quiet, and still, and solitary. The world will freely offer itself to you to be unmasked. It has no choice; it will roll in ecstasy at your feet."

If you're having difficulty coming up with new ideas, then slow down. For me, slowing down has been a tremendous source of creativity. It has allowed me to open up -- to know that there's life under the earth and that I have to let it come through me in a new way. Creativity exists in the present moment. You can't find it anywhere else.--Natalie Goldberg

Slow down and enjoy life. It's not only the scenery you miss by going too fast--you also miss the sense of where you are going and why.

Eddie Cantor

Biblical Quotes.

Phillipians 4: 6-7

1 Peter

Proverbs 3:5-6

Psalms 91: 1-16
"

Matthew 6:6

Luke 5:15-16

Luke 6: 12

Exodus 3: 1-2

Closing Thoughts. If you think you haven't the time to take some time, to slow down, and regenerate and rest, think again. Take time in small moments, and let them build up to become a regular part of your taking care and being more mindful and centered in your life. And think of Moses who was going about his business, or Mozart or Tesla, who took time to be quiet and alone....think of what wonderful ideas, visions, and messages are just waiting for you to have time for them to be noticed. Be at peace.

Notes:

"The prayer of the faithful is, 'Lord, show me my delusion.' The prayer of the faithless is, 'Lord, give me what I want.' It is the faithless that become extremists, not the faithful." – Fr. Antony

Recently, my Granddaughter and I were out Christmas shopping together in San Francisco. We had had a lot of fun finding little presents for our family, and had gone out to lunch together. We were walking down the street on our way to get an ice cream, when we passed the huge wooden doors of St. Patrick's Catholic Church on Folsom in downtown San Francisco. My Granddaughter asked me, "What's that?" The church is one of the oldest buildings in the neighborhood, and is dwarfed on all sides by large sky scrapers. It stands as a beautiful old ornate brick edifice amid a mass of modernity. I said, "That's St. Patrick's Church. Would you like to go in?" She replied, "I don't think so. I'm afraid." I said, "What are you afraid of?" She said, "I'm afraid there might be something really scary in there." I told her I understood, but said, "We could go in and see, and if there is anything that scares you, we can leave." She agreed, and we entered the church. Another of her favorite places is Mission Dolores where she loves to go whenever I am in town.

She recognized that it was similar, and there were people in the church preparing the altar for Christmas Eve, people praying, and street people taking shelter and finding a peaceful place to sit. My Granddaughter and I had a wonderful time watching the altar be filled with Poinsettias, the nativity scene being prepared for the baby Jesus who was not yet in the cradle. We spoke to one of the homeless ladies, and talked about the different icons and parts of the church. We got a candle and prayed for the Holy Family, our family, and all families together. What she had feared, was not part of our experience that Christmas Eve day. Being afraid is a natural part of our dealing with the unknown, the ambiguities of life, and of trying to maintain some balance and control over what happens to us in our lives. Undue fear, can hold us back from discovering beauty, joy, and deep happiness. It also holds us back from seeing what is really behind the doors that fear blocks us from entering.

How often do we let our fears lead us into false beliefs and distorted fantasies that have nothing to do with our essence and real lives? When we see it acted out on the world stage, we recognize it. When we see how others around us let fear direct their lives, we recognize the power they have given over to fear. When we ourselves are viewing life through the distortions of our own fear, however, it is often much more difficult to recognize.

What happens when we want to get control over our lives or surmount some kind of obstacle or challenging situation, is that we tend to look for reasons to explain why something is the way it is. We do this, sometimes, instead of listening to our emotional responses. Fear is one of those emotions that signals to us that we are feeling threatened, and we need some kind of protection. Fear can be a healthy response to a dangerous situation or a threatening experience or relationship.

Fear can also be a tyrant, used to fuel our 'worst case scenarios' and fantasies. When fear rises up in us, we may want to look at what we are afraid of. In facing our fears, we learn to see them for what they are. Creations of our own mind and imagination. The threat may be real, for example, you may have a fear that you have a physical situation that is getting worse and needs to be dealt with. On the other hand, to go from "I think I need to have that looked at" to "I'm going to have some life-threatening diagnosis and my life will change forever" is a giant leap, usually in the wrong direction.

Fears are signals—signals to an underlying threat of loss or being hurt, or discovering something that will upset you. For many, fear is a barrier, a roadblock to taking the next big step. We would sometimes rather live "in fear of" than to face the fear and see what is really involved. Years ago, I had a small growth on my arm. It had been there most of my life, and had never caused a problem. Within a period of a couple of years, it began to grow, until it got bigger and bigger. By the time I knew I had to find out what was going on, I had developed such a fear of what I might find out, that I was terrified when I finally went to the doctor. What I had built up in my head for quite some time, turned out to be unwarranted fear. The growth was a benign cyst that was taken care of within 15 minutes.

The initial fear, that something needed attending to, became an irrational fear when I failed to face the situation head on. We do this in all kinds of ways, and so for today, reflect on what it is you fear at this point in your life. What are you afraid of? What are you afraid to do or find out? What fears are in proportion to the source of the fear? What fears are out of proportion?

Consider one fear that has been with you for a while, and befriend it today. Talk to your fear, addressing it and trying to name it. "You are the unknown in a situation that has been important to me for a long time." "I'm afraid of what I might find out if I look more closely or ask for answers." Have whatever kind of conversation you need to have with your fear and see if you can use this experience to begin to face your fear.

Facing our fears requires that we develop our ability to be more courageous. How do we develop the ability to be courageous. According to neuroscientists, the portion of our brain that helps us think and act with more courage, is called the subgenual anterior singulate cortex (sgACC). Courage is more than facing fears; it is also about coping with risk taking and ambiguity/uncertainty.

Fears, especially those based on the unknown, require that we develop the ability to face our fears, name them, and then be willing to take the risk to discover what we can about the uncertainties in our lives. Strangely enough, our fears often center around opportunities, possibilities, and fabulous choices. Yes, we are often afraid of being happy, successful, creative, or productive. Some of our fears are based on difficult and challenging areas of our lives too, and yet learning to be courageous even in the worst of times, is a good survival mechanism. And it is certainly something that helps us grow emotionally, psychologically, mentally, and spiritually. So how do we do it?

Let yourself look upon your fears as signals or signs sent to you to guide you in a direction to help you. Even under the worst nightmare or irrational fear, there is a kernel of truth that is making its way into your consciousness. Something is not right and something needs to be done. The first step is becoming aware and allowing yourself to face that fear. I do a lot of dreamwork, and often hear people talking about nightmares they want to stop having. I myself have had some doozies, and understand the desire to forget the nightmare as quickly as possible. However, that is not what is meant to happen. When we get a terrible nightmare, it is a signal from our subconscious and often from the greater Collective Consciousness, that something needs attending to.

From our subconscious, arises our fears, hopes, passions, and needs. From the Collective Consciousness, comes direction, guidance, information, and a sense of what is going on in the world around us or in some area of spiritual development—usually all three. So for example, if you were to dream of being inundated by a giant wave breaking over you at sea, you might ask yourself, what in my life right now is like being overwhelmed and in danger of drowning? The more drastic the images in dreams, the more clarity is needed of one's own life, fears, and struggles.

How can we train ourselves to face our fears and be more courageous in acting on them? What happens when we are afraid?

Being afraid puts us in a position of feeling vulnerable. We often feel something will happen-to us, to someone else, to a situation. Facing fears means being willing to be vulnerable in order to find out the truth of the situation. Fear often is based on an idea that we are not worthy, not enough. Our fear is based on making ourselves vulnerable so that others see us in this state of not being enough. And what armor have we put on to protect ourselves from our own vulnerability? Rationalizing, intellectualizing, cynicism, fantasizing, or controlling? What is your armor when you feel vulnerable?

Acknowledging our fears is necessary. Getting the fear out of our bodies and into some form or shape. If we can't say what we are afraid of, we might start by drawing or painting it. Doodling may give you a way to begin opening yourself to the language you need to describe what it is you are afraid of. If you are considering a change of some sort, what is holding you back from making the change? If you are unhappy in a relationship, what fears are driving your choices and decisions? If you are wanting to start a new project or raise your own expectations for yourself, what are you afraid will happen if you take steps toward your goals? What's the worst that could happen? What's the best? Get the fear out of your head and into form. Name the fear so that it is not some giant amorphous entity that overwhelms you—remember the wave?

Expose yourself to what it is you fear. If you are afraid to dance, allow yourself to dance by yourself in your own home. Then give yourself permission to go somewhere where people are dancing and just watch for a while. Join a dance class. Take a dance class at your local college. Take small steps to desensitize yourself to something, and to learn how to embrace and overcome the fear.

In our relationships, we often need to gather the courage to face up to how we feel and to have the courage to talk about it. We might be afraid of what we are going to hear in return, but is the risk work it? If you want truly good communication it is. Good communication is based on being vulnerable, taking risks, and stating our truth. When we allow ourselves to do what feels difficult in broaching certain subjects, expressing needs, or discovering what someone else feels or believes, we have but one route—directly ahead over the fears and into the light of truth.

Be positive and optimistic. Consider how many of your fears are based in negative beliefs, thoughts, and past experiences. If a fear is based on something you have experienced, ask yourself, "What did I learn about myself and others through that experience?" We may have other choices or opportunities that seem similar, however, we are always learning. Each new experience we have can benefit from what we have learned from the past. Navigate as if you were going to reach your destination, and be willing to face any new challenges on your way. Be courageous, take a risk, and keep going. You won't find the pot at the end of the rainbow if you don't go looking for the rainbow.

Use your active imagination to visualize yourself succeeding, getting along with someone, reaching an agreement, or finding a solution. Whatever it is you are seeking, visualize it and act as if it were already a fact. It is just as easy to have a positive fantasy as it is to have a negative one. And if there is any truth to the idea that thoughts are energy, then the positive ones will do more to generate what you desire that the negative ones. Take a chance on being positive.

Another important part of facing fears is managing your stress. Fear and stress are often companions. Stress arises from imagined fears both emotional and physical. The results act themselves out in our bodies and minds, producing the release of stress hormones and other physiological reactions that are harmful to our health.   Both exercise and meditation have been proven effective for dealing with stress and anxiety. When you cope with your stress you are then more able to face and cope with your fears. Before taking steps toward something that you find fearful, go into meditation or prayer, and find some stillness. Ask for guidance, and then rest in the assurance that "there is a right thing to do, you know what it is, and you know you can do it." That little prayer is my battle cry—one my Mother taught me when I was a young girl.

Practice acts of courage. Nothing ever gets done without an element of courage. You have already lived courageously in your life. Think of the battles you have won, the mountains you have climbed, and the obstacles you have overcome to be who you are where you are now. If nothing comes to mind, spend some time today thinking about all the really difficult times you have had when you thought you wouldn't make it. What got you through? What did you learn? When did you open a door that you thought might be scary, only to find a treasure waiting for you? There are treasures yet to be discovered by you. Get out there and open some of those doors.

Inspriational Quotes:

"The love of God, unutterable and perfect, flows into a pure soul the way light rushes into a transparent object. The more love that it finds, the more it gives itself: so that, as we grow clear and open, the more complete the joy of heaven is.And the more souls who resonate together, the greater the intensity of their love, and, mirror-like, each soul reflects the other.
- Dante

Unconditional --Jennifer Welwood

Opening to my loss
Willing to experience aloneness,
I discover connection everywhere;
Turning to face my fear,
I meet the warrior who lives within;
I gain the embrace of the universe;
Surrendering into emptiness,
I find fullness without end.
Each condition I flee from pursues me,
Each condition I welcome transforms me
And becomes itself transformed
Into its radiant jewel-like essence.
I bow to the one who has made it so,
Who has crafted this Master Game;
To play it is purest delight;
To honor it's form – true devotion.

Fear keeps us focused on the past or worried about the future. If we can acknowledge our fear, we can realize that right now we are okay. Right now, today, we are still alive, and our bodies are working marvelously. Our eyes can still see the beautiful sky. Our ears can still hear the voices of our loved ones."--Thich Nhat Hanh

Too many of us are not living our dreams because we are living our fears. ~Les Brown

Ultimately we know deeply that the other side of every fear is freedom. ~Mary Ferguson

"Our deepest fear is not that we are inadequate. Our deepest fear is that we are powerful beyond measure. It is our light, not our darkness, that most frightens us. We ask ourselves, Who am I to be brilliant, gorgeous, talented, fabulous? Actually, who are you not to be? You are a child of God. Your playing small does not serve the world. There is nothing enlightened about shrinking so that other people won't feel insecure around you. We are all meant to shine, as children do. We were born to make manifest the glory of God that is within us. It's not just in some of us; it's in everyone. And as we let our own light shine, we unconsciously give other people permission to do the same. As we are liberated from our own fear, our presence automatically liberates others." ~ Marianne Williamson

"Let me not pray to be sheltered from dangers, but to be fearless in facing them. Let me not beg for the stilling of my pain, but for the heart to conquer it." ~ Tagore

"Fear defeats more people than any other one thing in the world." ~ Ralph Waldo Emerson

"You gain strength, courage and confidence by every experience in which you really stop to look fear in the face. You are able to say to yourself, 'I have lived through this horror. I can take the next thing that comes along.' You must do the thing you think you cannot do." ~ Eleanor Roosevelt

"There is no illusion greater than fear."
— Lao Tzu

"Nothing in life is to be feared. It is only to be understood.'--Marie Curie

"Our job is to love others without stopping to inquire whether or not they are worthy. That is not our business and, in fact, it is nobody's business. What we are asked to do is to love, and this love itself will render both ourselves and our neighbors worthy." -Thomas Merton

Biblical Quotes:

Psalms 27:1

2 Timothy 1:7

Psalms 56:3-4

Isaiah 41:10

Isaiah 41:13

Isaiah 54: 4

1 John 4:18

Notes:

Corinthians 6: 19,20. Reminds us of our divine nature: "What? know ye not that your body is the temple of the Holy Spirit [which is] in you, which ye have of God, and ye are not your own?

20 For ye are bought with a price: therefore glorify God in your body, and in your spirit, which are God's."

Sometimes we forget not only that we have Divine gifts, but also that we are Divine and reflection of that Divinity. We get so caught up in meeting basic needs and feeling that it is up to just us to handle everything that needs to be done. Let's take some time today to reflect on that spiritual nature that is our true grounding and our basic need. We are infused with that Divine energy, and it is up to us to use it and understand it as the gift that it is...not to be squandered or distorted, but to be used to be fruitful, to be loving and kind, and to love and be loved in return.

For the final seven days of our Retreat-in-Daily Life, we will look at the different types of energy that we experience each day as part of our journey as spiritual beings having a physical experience. Each of us is infused with a unique, individual set of qualities, skills, talents, temperment, and purpose. Our lives are all about living in awareness of how that beautiful essence of what makes us who we are gets along with others and lives out the purpose inherent within this experience.

Our human body is much more than a random set of bone, organs, chemical and hormonal soup--we are infused with energy and a consciousness that allows us to compose, create, observe, reason, love, and express ourselves in countless ways. Our energy system composes our subtle or auric body where the energy channels (nadis) meet to carry energy/our life force/ Chi/Prana throughout our body. Where energy gathers in our bodies, our life force/energy pools/vortexes of energy that are connected to our emotions, thoughts, feelings, memories, beliefs, psychological, and spiritual
spiritual identity.

We are connected, body, mind, and spirit to all that has ever happened to us, to our surroundings and interactions, and to our conscious and subconscious thoughts, beliefs, memories, and ideas.

Our physical health is also affected by how we express, process, and cope with the different experiences of our lives. Most of us recognize that we are affected by our upbringing, our environment, our relationships, and our our own unique experience of life. Two people who are raised under very difficult and abusive conditions, make very different choices about how they live their lives.

Our circumstances do not define us; we humans have both consciousness (an awareness of how we are acting and what we are feeling and believing) and and choice (personal volition to decide how to view circumstance and respond or react to the experiences we are engaged in). That is not to say that we always feel like we have choice or that we are free to escape difficult circumstances and challenges (even tragedies or conditions inherent in the cultures in which we live). It does, however, give us a perspective and ability to reason and respond differently than others might.

Just for today, consider what it is that tends to ground you and make you feel more or less at home with yourself. Where do you feel at home? What places have been more homelike for you, and where have you felt ungrounded and out of place?

Just for today, consider what beliefs and experiences from childhood or your earlier life have left a lasting impression on who you are now. Are there belief patterns that seem to come from your family and home? What unfinished business do you have with your family? What is the personal code of honor you have developed for yourself?

Just for today, consider all the blessings you have from your family of origin, and/or from the family you have helped create. The older we get, the more our idea of family changes.

Just for today, contemplate how you have remain affected by unresolved grief and sorrow, or abuse or lack from the past. Some of us, however, still carry around a lot of unresolved pain and grief from our earliest childhood and youth. Notice if any unresolved issues continue to connect you to earlier experiences.

Just for today, consider the gifts you have from your family connections, and contemplate how some of the sorrow, sadness, or blessings have taught you something about your own strengths and gifts. What is your experience of coping with stressful and hurtful situations?

Just for today, consider how you might block your own happiness and creativity. What is your experiences of dealing with opportunities and creative challenges? What are your thoughts on your own worthiness? Do you sometimes not feel 'good enough' or 'smart enough' or strong enough to do what you want or need to do?

Spend a little time noticing how and when you feel challenged to cope with life experiences, and when you feel energized and motivated to meet challenges, accept opportunities, and take risks that might lead you to some positive changes?

Our spiritual journey is often not about overcoming the odds or simply 'getting over' what has happened in the past. It is more often about being willing to take some steps toward accepting risks and heading out into unfamiliar and uncertain territory.

What would you like to do next, and what seems to be stopping you from moving towards that goal?

Words of Inspiration.

"You cannot swim for new horizons until you have courage to lose sight of the shore."
— William Faulkner

"A ship is safe in harbor, but that's not what ships are for."
— William G.T. Shedd
"Happiness is a risk. If you're not a little scared, then you're not doing it right."
— Sarah Addison Allen, The Peach Keeper

"Risk anything! Care no more for the opinion of others ... Do the hardest thing on earth for you. Act for yourself. Face the truth."

(Journal entry, 14 October 1922)"
— Katherine Mansfield, Journal of Katherine Mansfield

"When you walk to the edge of all the light you have and take that first step into the darkness of the unknown, you must believe that one of two things will happen. There will be something solid for you to stand upon or you will be taught to fly."
— Patrick Overton, The leaning tree: [poems]

"A bend in the road is not the end of the road…Unless you fail to make the turn."
— Helen Keller

"Pitiful is the person who is afraid of taking risks. Perhaps this person will never be disappointed or disillusioned; perhaps she won't suffer the way people do when they have a dream to follow. But when that person looks back – and at some point everyone looks back – she will hear her heart saying, "What have you done with the miracles that God planted in your days? What have you done with the talents God bestowed on you? You buried yourself in a cave because you were fearful of losing those talents. So this is your heritage; the certainty that you wasted your life."
— Paulo Coelho, By the River Piedra I Sat Down and Wept

Biblical Quotations.

Solomon 2:12

Solomon 8:6

Ecclesiastes   11: 4-6

Matthew 25:14-30

Ecclesiastes 11: 1-3

Deuteronomy 31:6

Romans 8:28

Notes:

Psychologist Williams James once remarked, "We are like islands in the sea, separate on the surface but connected in the deep."

Our ability to connect with and feel empathy and compassion for another person, is one of our most spiritual and creative gifts. With the energy we generate in relationships, we build beautiful monuments, paint masterpieces, write classic literature, and epic poetry. With the energy we share through our connections with those we love, we form life-long bonds, deep and lasting friendships, and strong connections that last through the best and worst of times.

As part of our 40-day retreat-in-daily life, we have been spending time allowing ourselves time during our busy lives and normal routines. We have been taking just a little bit of time away from the routine, special times, individual and family emergencies, crises, or events. During the past 40 days, we have celebrated holy days, lost loved ones to death, celebrated births, become engaged or married, or have celebrated great turning points in our lives. Some of us have been traveling, and exploring new places or revisiting home and family after many years away. Some of us haven't had much of a break from our work, while others of us have been able to take more time to 'retreat' than usual due to winter breaks and holiday schedules.

Regardless of how you have been able to participate and use this experience, we are all seeking time, meaning, and ways to better understand who we are, what our connections and relationships touch and demand of us, and how our experiences of life challenge, connect, and inspire us to grow in love, compassion, and creativity.

Just for today, consider where you feel connections in life. What places inspire and nourish you? What kinds of surroundings make you feel more at home than others? Which relationships are growing and nourishing you as a person, and which ones do you find draining or challenging? Are there any connections you maintain that seem to be crumbling, despite your efforts? Are there connections in the places where you spend your time that are not healthy? Give yourself permission to observe what is working in your life, and what needs to be cleaned up, fixed, nourished, or eliminated or changed in some fashion.

Just for today consider how you have been inspired and motivated by your religious and spiritual beliefs and practices in the past. You may have left a tradition, but still long for aspects of that tradition in your life right now. What about the past (traditions, rituals, service opportunities, community, and worship) do you miss?

Just for today, consider what needs to be tuned up in your life. Our automobiles need to be maintained, and though we are not mechanical beings, we too need ongoing monitoring and maintenance. What do your current spiritual and/or religious practices look like? What is missing? Where do you feel disconnected?

What would you like to add to your daily practices? What would you like to eliminate? Are you simply 'going through the motions' with some behavior and habits? If so, how could you change either or both to reflect a more life-affirming and uplifting element of what you are seeking?

Just for today, think back on how your beliefs and ideas about your spiritual nature, the Divine, and the connection between your ideas and your own life practices have changed over time. How do your current practices support the issues, challenges, needs and desires of your life right now? Are your ideas and beliefs, your perspectives and attitudes congruent with your actions, daily life, routines, habits, and patterns of behavior? Does your work and art reflect who you are? How do your friendships affirm or challenge you as a person?

Just for today consider how your are creating connections, and experiencing the kinds of relationships you need to sustain and affirm you. In your meditations and through your prayers, seek for signs, answers, and guidance for what you are missing, what you might need to change, or what is calling for your attention. Where are the growing edges for you in life right now? We often develop our practices and beliefs amid times of crisis or over long periods of time when the demands of our lives require that we find some way of seeking support, connection, guidance, and ways of coping with stress, difficult situations, or chronic challenges of one kind or another. For example, we may have been supporting a loved one through an emergency or chronic illness. We may have been the caregiver for an aging and dying parent or other family member. We may have been working on a long project (an academic degree, a training, or the demands of a job), and find now, a point of change and relief.

Just for today, take one step in the direction of adding a life-affirming practice to you life. You do not need to make a life-long commitment to it, but what is one small change you could make just for today, that would give you a greater sense of spiritual connection, meaning, or purpose?

Words of Inspiration.

"Love is our true destiny. We do not find the meaning of life by ourselves alone - we find it with another."
— Thomas Merton, Love and Living

"You and I know spiritually about belonging, leaving, and returning. We, like the young prodigal, can learn to act ahead of our feelings, trust that love is there, and make our shaky return."
--Henri Nouwen

"One love, one heart, one destiny."
— Bob Marley

"Do stuff. be clenched, curious. Not waiting for inspiration's shove or society's kiss on your forehead. Pay attention. It's all about paying attention. attention is vitality. It connects you with others. It makes you eager. stay eager."
— Susan Sontag

"I define connection as the energy that exists between people when they feel seen, heard, and valued; when they can give and receive without judgment; and when they derive sustenance and strength from the relationship."
— Brené Brown

"If we have no peace, it is because we have forgotten that we belong to each other."
— Mother Teresa

"Love and compassion are necessities, not luxuries. Without them, humanity cannot survive."
— Dalai Lama XIV, The Art of Happiness

"A dream you dream alone is only a dream. A dream you dream together is reality."
— John Lennon

"When we give cheerfully and accept gratefully, everyone is blessed."
— Maya Angelou

"When we know ourselves to be connected to all others, acting compassionately is simply the natural thing to do. "
— Rachel Naomi Remen

"If your daily life seems poor, do not blame it; blame yourself, tell yourself that you are not poet enough to call forth its riches; for to the creator there is no poverty and no poor indifferent place."
— Rainer Maria Rilke, Letters to a Young Poet

The creation of the world did not take place once and for all time, but takes place every day."
— Samuel Beckett, Proust

Because you're a creation of God, you reflect the Divine qualities of creativity, wisdom, and love."
— Doreen Virtue
"God has created you, not your future."
— Amit Kalantri

Story is the umbilical cord that connects us to the past, present, and future. Family. Story is a relationship between the teller and the listener, a responsibility. . . . Story is an affirmation of our ties to one another."
— Terry Tempest Williams, Pieces of White Shell

"We often forget our human connectedness. Throughout my life, I have felt the greatest beauty lies in this connection. It has been in the deepest connections with others that I have experienced the greatest degree of learning, healing and transformation. This connection is a

powerful thing, with the ability to transform lives, and ultimately transform human experience."
— Kristi Bowman, Journey to One: A Woman's Story of Emotional Healing and Spiritual Awakening

"The history of your happiness is the history of your feeling connected."
— Vironika Tugaleva, The Love Mindset

"You are never alone. You are eternally connected with everyone."
— Amit Ray

Biblical and Spiritual Quotations.

Colossians 1: 9-10

Matthew 5:6

Phillipians 4:13

Hebrews 10: 23

James 1: 2-4

Galatians 5:22-23

Matthew 6:33

Notes:

Have you ever been in a frightening situation, and felt a gut wrenching feeling in your solar plexus region? Or do you recall seeing someone who is scared, holding their hands and arms across their midsection, in a protective stance? The Solar Plexus area of the body, is a part of us, like our entire body, that is constantly giving us information and sending us signals about ourselves and our surroundings.

When taking a self defense course, a good friend told me her instructor told everyone in the class, the most important tool you have for self defense is your instincts and intuition. Always trust your instinctive feelings. In ancient traditions, this area of the energy body is call the third chakra. The third chakra, located in the region of the Solar Plexus, is called Manipura. This is the energy of our system that governs digestion and the processes of metabolism. It is also the place in the body where the energy of will, motivation, and instincts is centered.

Our intuitive right brain is always 'reading' the energy in and around us, picking up the subtle messages of from the environment storing it to be processed with the rational mind. It is the seat of well being and security in our physical body, and it is an important part of our ability to maintain greater awareness of what is going on both within and around us.

Gut instincts, or that inner knowing that arises from the area in and around the solar plexus, carries with it a tangible and physical energy that feels like a 'nervous stomach', butterflies in our stomach, and often somatic stomach or belly aches. Somatic pain or distress is a very real pain rooted in mental, emotional, or psychological anguish or upset.

Our gut instincts are not only signal us but also deliver important information to us about our own state of well being, safety, security, and inner truth. When we notice pain or discomfort in this area, it is often due to some threat, real or perceived, that we need to pay attention to. We want to trust our gut instincts as they are the early warning signals of our psycho-biological body.

What good are gut instincts?

Gut instincts often signal to us that there is something amiss in our physical body. Your body is like a geiger counter for picking up and reading the energy in and around you. When there is something wrong in our physical body, we often know first through our intuitive senses. "Something is not quite right. Something just doesn't feel right," are what you might say or hear someone say.

Dreams often give us indications of threats to our physical health. They can be useful if we pay attention. In a dream I had years ago, I dreamed my car was speeding along with me at the wheel, when all of a sudden my back, right tire blew out, and my car skidded to a screeching halt and veered off the road. My first thought when exploring the dream was to check my car, which I did.

This dream occurred at a time when my schedule was packed and I was pushing myself and doing more than I needed to be do. Within a day or two of the dream, I fell and injured my right leg. The injury caused my life to change drastically. I could no longer keep up the pace I had been keeping, nor could I do all the activities that I had been doing. "Stopped in my tracks" and "veering of my course" became reality for me.

When we pay attention to our gut instincts, another form of intuitive knowledge, we often 'hear' or sense the warnings we need to protect ourselves or to become aware of something that is not quite right in our physical body. For example, when we suddenly feel drained of energy when near a certain person or place or in certain conditions (crowds, enclosed spaces, unfamiliar locations, or simply walking into a room), we are being shown through that intuition that something in the environment is draining energy.

When you are around someone or in certain circumstances and your energy suddenly goes down, that is your intuition telling you something is amiss. This experience is your body's way of letting you know something or someone is draining your energy.

We can also feel intuitive or gut feelings in other ways. We may feel burning sensations in our stomach, or in our chest. Our skin may feel like it is crawling, or we may get chills up and down our spines. These are all the brain's way of warning us that something is threatening to us. It is important to pay attention to this kind of intuition, even if we don't understand it. A nagging suspicion can be an indication that we are sensing an imbalance or disturbance in our health-- it's important to follow up with doubts that relate to our health and well being. Intuition is like a second brain that demands to be listened to in order to protect your health and security.

This 'gut feeling' also signals to us when we know what is true for us, but don't necessarily want to do anything to change our behavior.

When in crisis situations, it is also important to listen to our intuition. Within the first few seconds of being in a new situation or meeting a person, our instincts kick in to let us know whether or not we feel safe. Our instincts are important for survival and protection, however we have to be careful how we respond for we also let our beliefs, experiences, and fears enter into the picture when we are in new or crisis-like situations.

We have to learn to pay attention to instincts, and to respond in ways that are not going to cause more harm to ourselves or others. For example, running away or moving away from a dangerous situation or a person who you perceive as threatening is crucial. Attacking or confronting such a person is not, and in fact can cause greater harm.

Our instincts and intuition also help us to sense when someone needs helps. Our ability to empathize and feel compassion for another person, also enables us to be sympathetic towards someone who may need help. We can share a smile or reassuring word or two to someone who is nervous on an airplane or who is feeling at a loss. This works differently depending on the situation. In my small town, when someone appears to be lost on the street, it is considered neighborly to provide some reassurance and help--giving directions or suggestions.

To do the same thing in a big city, like San Francisco, the response on the street to trying to help or make a suggestion to a stranger can be met with very different reactions. In a city, in some cases, a stranger could be perceived as a threat rather than a help. We have to use our discretion in such situations, but that is part of the instinctual response as well. Making choices based on what we feel or intuit rather than on what we necessarily know.

For many people, the gut instinct to want to be helpful is a powerful motivator, and is something that makes us feel good. We often sense someone needs help, and it feels good when we can offer something to assist another. Practicing generosity generally makes us feel better about ourselves in addition to helping someone else. If we over do, neglecting our own self care or using our generosity to manipulate, then we cross the line from helping another to using them for our own gratification.

Another area of our lives when operating on instinct is better than depending on rational thought is when we are doing something that we know how to do well. Research shows that when first learning to do something, like learn a language, drive a car, or learn a new skill, the rational mind is put to good use. I was trying to explain to my sister how to do something on the internet that I know how to do really well. It was almost impossible for me, for I do it instinctively now. To try to break it down into steps is very difficult. When we're driving, we do not drive as if we were just learning, trying to remember when to put our foot on the brake, clutch, or gas pedal and when to turn or signal.After we learned it, it became instinctual. To over think a skill we already know, gets in the way of doing it well. What are some things you do instinctively, and what things are you still learning to do?

And for those of us who over think the choices we make in relationships, career or education, or other life-changing decisions, the research suggests that the best choices are made by following your instincts. This may be why a friend who spends months telling you all the reasons they should or should not stay in a relationship is probably better off following their gut instinct about what they feel is right for them; rational decisions about emotional, psychological and spiritual choices tend not to be as satisfying or fulfilling.

Our instincts tell us what we really feel or want and not what sounds good or fits some ideal or fantasy that we hold in our thinking. I notice when I spend too much time over thinking a decision or choice, I am operating out of fear. Fear of feeling capable, or fear of finding out the truth, or fear of something that might block me from being safe, secure, or happy.

Our spiritual journey is often a battle between the rational and instinctual needs we have. Much more of our lives are governed by and experienced through our senses, instincts, intuition, and emotions than through the mental images and beliefs we have. Our thoughts are energy and help create the attitudes, perspectives, and beliefs that we view the world through-- the lens and eye on the world. Yet our intuition and imagination inform us. We receive information, ideas, inspiration, and we make connections through our intuitive senses. Together they work beautifully together, blending the best of both into a cohesive, congruent experience of life.

Just for today, spend some time allowing yourself to be more mindful of your intuitive senses. Allow yourself to follow a hunch, or be led by an instinctual urge to do something differently.

Just for today, notice what your intuition, instincts, and senses tell you about your environment, about the people you meet in different places, and about how you feel in different areas of your home, your life, and in relationships. Notice what is energizing, enlightening, and engaging, and what is not. Contemplate what is is you really want and need, and then observe for yourself, whether or not your life right now reflects that.

In your meditative and prayer practices, notice how you feel connected to the Divine. What feels and is experienced as sacred time and space in your daily life? How do your spirituality and religious ideals play themselves out in your daily life? What do you listen for, watch, or pay attention to when you seek Divine guidance? What do you need more of right now, to strengthen, deepen, or infuse more purpose and meaning in your life?

Enjoy letting yourself be led and guided to day, and listen for that 'still small voice' and see how it shows up to help you, guide you, inspire you, or connect you in ways you need for greater purpose and meaning. Allow yourself to become more aware of what intuition is experienced as physical sensation, emotional signals, mental images and messages, psychological knowing or understanding, or whatever ways you experience the growing awareness of how the sacred is you and your life.

Our lives are based on how we experience faith and grace. Faith to not have to know or know all the answers or reasons why. Grace given to us freely, whether we ask for it or not, whether we deserve it or not, and grace given freely in the course of daily life as we allow our true essence to flow freely in simply being who we are and sharing our lives with those who we love and who love us. In that cycle of giving and receiving love, we give an receive the essence of Life--that is truly sacred.

Trust yourself to receive what you need for your happiness and fulfillment. Trust that you know what you need, want, and believe to be true. Trust that you have within your grasps, the questions, the answers, and the gifts you need to live a perfectly beautiful life, being you.

Biblical Quotations.

Proverbs 2:1-5

Proverbs 18:15

Hebrews 4:12

1 Corinthians 14:33

1 Corinthians 12: 8-10

Words of Inspiration.

"I have been and still am a seeker, but I have ceased to question stars and books; I have begun to listen to the teaching my blood whispers to me." --Hermann Hesse

"Instinct is a marvelous thing. It can neither be explained nor ignored." --Agatha Christie

"In art as in love, instinct is enough. " --Anatole France

"Yoga says instinct is a trace of an old experience that has been repeated many times and the impressions have sunk down to the bottom of the mental lake. Although they go down, they aren't completely erased. Don't think you ever forget anything. All experiences are stored in the chittam; and, when the proper atmosphere is created, they come to the surface again. When we do something several times it forms a habit. Continue with that habit for a long time, and it becomes your character. Continue with that character and eventually, perhaps in another life, it comes up as instinct. (92)"
— Swami Satchidananda, The Yoga Sutras

"I believe in intuitions and inspirations...I sometimes FEEL that I am right. I do not KNOW that I am."
— Albert Einstein

"Intuition is seeing with the soul."
— Dean Koontz

"Our bodies have five senses: touch, smell, taste, sight, hearing. But not to be overlooked are the senses of our souls: intuition, peace, foresight, trust, empathy. The differences between people lie in their use of these senses; most people don't know anything about the inner senses while a few people rely on them just as they rely on their physical senses, and in fact probably even more."
— C. JoyBell C.

"What a lover's heart knows let no man's brain dispute."
— Aberjhani, Visions of a Skylark Dressed in Black

"intuition is always right in at least two important ways;
It is always in response to something.
it always has your best interest at heart"
— Gavin de Becker

The intuitive mind is a sacred gift and the rational mind is a faithful servant. We have created a society that honors the servant and has forgotten the gift. We will not solve the problems of the world from the same level of thinking we were at when we created them. More than anything else, this new century demands new thinking: We must change our materially based analyses of the world around us to include broader, more multidimensional perspectives."
— Albert Einstein

"We always know which is the best road to follow, but we follow only the road that we have become accustomed to."
— Paulo Coelho

"The truth about life and lie about life is not measured by others but by your intuition, which never lies."
— Santosh Kalwar

"Intuition comes in several forms:
- a sudden flash of insight, visual or auditory
- a predictive dream
- a spinal shiver of recognition as something is occurring or told to you
- a sense of knowing something already
- a sense of deja vu
- a snapshot image of a future scene or event
- knowledge, perspective or understanding divined from tools which respond to the subconscious mind"
— Sylvia Clare

"You must train your intuition - you must trust the small voice inside you which tells you exactly what to say, what to decide."
— Ingrid Bergman

"Nothing comes unannounced, but many can miss the announcement. So it's very important to actually listen to your own intuition rather than driving through it."
— Terence McKenna

Meditation is an essential travel partner on your journey of personal transformation. Meditation connects you with your soul,and this connection gives you access to your intuition, your heartfelt desires, your integrity, and the inspiration to create a life you love."
— Sarah McLean

"The truth is that you are already the perfect embodiment of love. It is who you are deep within." Panache Desai

Some days you wake up and simply breathing is enough to remind you of what a gift life is. Some days the truth of that spills out of each moment, right at your feet, delivered as if it were a direct message from the Divine. Notice today how you are the perfect embodiment of Love.

Within each of us, is that deep well of desire, purpose, love, and meaning that longs to rise up and become part of how we live and move, and have our being. We often hold in our hearts, our deepest desires, protecting and guarding them for fear they will never be allowed to be expressed or lived out. Within our hearts we store our grief, disappointments, longings, and aching for the perfect time, conditions, or opportunities to present themselves so we can release the desire and love that is trapped within.

Following our hearts does not mean acting without regard for others or without using our powers of reason and intellect. Just the opposite. To fully function from a Spirit and Heart-based center, we need to be constantly becoming aware of all aspects of our being--body, mind, emotions, spirit. We need to be using our experiences and training and talents to inspire, support, nourish, and drive ourselves and others as well. The more we are paying attention, the greater likelihood there is that we will be following our hearts.

Everything goes together. Our heart lets us know on a physical, emotional, psychological, spiritual, and intellectual level just what the health of our body is. Physically, what are you doing to nourish, take care of, and support your body's physical well being? How are you eating? What kinds of exercise, rest, and relaxation are you giving it? How are you taking care of your health and well being? What needs repair and greater support?

Emotionally, how are you tending to your feelings and levels of stress? What kinds of stressors are in your daily life, and how do you manage them? What kinds of stress is draining your body and activating stress hormones in unhealthy ways? What can you do about that? How do your emotions affect you on a day to day basis, and which ones are more likely than not, to be primary? What kinds of chronic or long-term experiences are causing you to tax your emotional strength? Doing exercise and meditating is just like putting a band aid on a broken bone. You need to do what you can to heal that which is broken. Continuing to re-injure ourselves, either emotionally or physically, is going to do more damage in the long run. What needs addressing?

Our emotions are connected to other areas of our being. What psychological parts of your being need healing or readjusting? How are your behaviors, instincts, patterns of thinking, and personality traits affecting the life you are living? What are you ignoring or trying to forget about who you are? Our personalities and temperment, combined with experiences, subconscious needs, socialization, and habits, incline us in certain directions, but in no way destine or doom us. We have the capacity to act, change, alter, and redirect ourselves in ways that are healthier and more life-affirming. We also have capacity to do the opposite. As our retreat-in-daily life is nearing its completion, consider what matters most right now, for setting your direction and course from this point.

A major function of spending some time in retreat, any kind of retreat, is to become more mindful of who you are, what your life, your body, and your entire being is telling you what you need to know. The more we listen, observe, pay attention to our thoughts, our intuition and hunches, to signs and symbols that catch our attention, to advice we take or reject, and to just how the daily life events and relationships we are already in, the closer we will come to knowing what it is we are meant to notice. Just as our dreams jolt us to make us pay attention and take action to change something that is a threat, so too do our observations, our feelings, emotions, relationships, and all the challenges and obstacles we face. We often get sick at a point when we most need to take time to take better care of ourselves...however, there is usually something beneath the illness or injury that is calling to be noticed.

Take some time today, and listen to what you need and desire. If you could live your life the way that you believe would be living out your highest good and purpose, what would it look like? What would have to change? What is stopping you from moving in that direction? What could you do today to take a little bit better care of yourself? What is calling for more attention?

Take steps to feed your body, mind, heart, and soul today.

Ask yourself today, what emotional memories do I need to heal?

What current relationships, present or past, need healing?

What emotional wounds still need healing, and how might those wounds be causing me to try to control other people or situations or causing me to feel victimized?

How do I let other peoples wounds, situations, or needs control me?

And a big one for our heart, how do I need to forgive myself and others? Who do I need forgiveness from?

Biblical Quotations.

Luke 12: 34 For where your treasure is, there will your heart be also.

Proverbs 3: 5-7   Trust in the Lord with all your heart, and do not lean on your own understanding. In all your ways acknowledge him, and he will make straight your paths. Be not wise in your own eyes; fear the Lord, and turn away from evil.

Matthew 6:22 "The eye is the lamp of the body. So, if your eye is healthy, your whole body will be full of light."

I Corinthians 15:44 It is sown a natural body; it is raised a spiritual body. If there is a natural body, there is also a spiritual body.

Inspirational Quotes.

"Put your mind, heart, and soul into even your smallest acts. That is the true secret of success."
Swami Sivananda

"Let yourself be silently drawn by the strange pull of what you really love. It will not lead you astray."
— Rumi, The Essential Rumi

"To know how to choose a path with heart is to learn how to follow intuitive feeling. Logic can tell you superficially where a path might lead to, but it cannot judge whether your heart will be in it."
— Jean Shinoda Bolen

"Speech is the voice of the heart."
— Anna Quindlen

Today's theme asks you to consider how you communicate who you are to others. Reflect today on how you talk to yourself and about yourself. Spend some time considering the stories you tell about who you are.

Take some time today to contemplate some of the questions that we need to ask about our sense of balance in self expression and communication.

What are you keeping to yourself that you long to share or express?

What are you afraid or worried to talk about?

What feelings or opinions are you afraid to talk about?

Are you in any way feeling not free to be yourself and express yourself?

What truths are you afraid to admit to yourself? What do you withhold

from others?

What are you longing to say? To whom?

In what ways are you feeling you hold back from expressing or being yourself?

What kinds of physical, emotional, or others types of aches and pains or issues are causing you stress or discomfort? What seems to be out of balance? What seems to be running smoothly? What helps bring you back into balance?

Spend some time to day assessing what it is you need to regain balance in your life. Maybe you need some extra sleep, or need to take better care of yourself. Perhaps you need more exercise, or need to recuperate and heal from some type of injury or illness.

How are you nourishing yourself? How can you use your voice to bring yourself into greater harmony?

Who do you need to forgive?

Listen to how you talk to and about yourself, and see if you can discover some of the messages you inadvertently are reinforcing (i.e., "I don't have time to rest," "I can't afford to take a day off", or "I have so much to do, I have to stay up late again." Simply notice what you reinforce in your self talk, and then listen to what you tell others about who you are.

Be mindful about how you tell your story, and what you have made the priorities in your life. Notice what works well as well as what does not.

Spend a little time asking yourself what you believe to be true about yourself, who you are as a sacred being, and what you believe the Divine wants, expects, desires, or needs for you. Ask the questions that you feel are important to you right now, and be mindful of how the answers come to you.

Notice how you are being treated and how others treat you.

Treat yourself like a special guest today, and prepare everything as if you want everything to be just perfect for the visit, the time you spend with your guest, yourself. Put some chocolates on your own pillow tonight, give yourself a little special attention. When we nourish and tend to ourselves, we are refreshed and able to share the same kindness and love with others.

Biblical Inspiration.

Phillipians 4: 8-9 Finally, brothers and sisters, whatever is true, whatever is honorable, whatever is just, whatever is pure, whatever is lovely, whatever is commendable, if there is any excellence, if there is anything worthy of praise, think about these things. What you have learned and received and heard and seen in me—practice these things, and the God of peace will be with you.

Hebrews 11: 1 Now faith is the assurance of things hoped for, the conviction of things not seen.

Words of Inspiration.

"The privilege of a lifetime is to become who you truly are."   Carl Jung

"Authenticity is a collection of choices that we have to make every day. It's about the choice to show up and be real. The choice to be honest. The choice to let our true selves be seen." — Brené Brown

"This above all: to thine own self be true,
And it must follow, as the night the day,
Thou canst not then be false to any man." --William Shakespeare

"A bird doesn't sing because it has an answer, it sings because it has a song." – Maya Angelou

"Shhhhhhhh..... Be silent. Silence your mind and listen.... Let the voice of your soul echo and shiiiiine!" — Angie Karan Krises

"Few are those who see with their own eyes and feel with their own hearts." -Albert Einstein

"What is the finding of love,
but a voice answering a voice?"
— D. Antoinette Foy

"Simple, genuine goodness is the best capital to found the business of this life upon. It lasts when fame and money fail, and is the only riches we can take out of this world with us."— Louisa May Alcott

"A wonderful fact to reflect upon, that every human creature is constituted to be that profound secret and mystery to every other." —Charles Dickens

"It's called an inner voice for a reason. It's the gnawing feeling inside your stomach telling you yes or no. It is the one voice in your life that is not tampered by other's biased opinions, scars, feelings or thoughts. Go with it, you know yourself better than anyone ever does."
— Hope Alcocer

"It is good to have an end to journey toward, but it is the journey that matters in the end."
— Ursula K. Le Guin

In Closing:

This 40-day Retreat-in-Daily Life has been a journey, that is drawing to its close. When you commit to spending some time each day focusing on your spiritual journey, and taking time to devote to discerning how you are drawing closer to the Divine in the course of your daily lives, you are creating a spiritual practice. However you have used this experience, you have followed a path to a point of completion.

Whether you have been able to do the retreat daily, or whether you have done it when you could, the point is, you have experienced a retreat-in-daily life, and have experienced special gifts, graces, and blessings. What matters most is how you experienced the journey itself, and what you have experienced that you can take with you as you move beyond the framework of this retreat.

For the last two days of the retreat, spend some time contemplating what you have enjoyed most, what has been frustrating or discouraging for you, and how the overall experience has affected the way you live each day.
What have you discovered? What have you overcome? How have you used this experience to support your daily life?

Just for today, ponder how you usually feel about endings and completions.

Just for today, notice the pace of your life, and some of the small changes that you may have made over the last 40 days.

Just for today, consider two or three ideas, experiences, or practices you would like to carry forward with you as you move on from this part of your journey?

Just for today, consider how you have deepened your own sense of spirituality during this time. How have you felt called to change, move, deepen, or become more open to some aspect of spiritual development?

Spend some time simply letting the course of the last 39-40 days (or whatever length of time you have taken to engage in this spiritual journey) be what they have been. Imagine you are going to pick a bouquet of ideas, thoughts, activities, awarenesses, inspiration, and prayers to remember this retreat by. What would that bouquet be like?

Biblical Quotes.

Psalm 119:105 (Remember Word in ancient times meant the voice of the Divine to be discerned, dreamed, and received through signs, symbols, obstacles, insight, and intuition.)

Psalm 121: 8

Exodus 13: 21

Matthew 6: 25-34

Matthew 11: 28

Inspirational Words.
"It is always important to know when something has reached its end. Closing circles, shutting doors, finishing chapters, it doesn't matter what we call it; what matters is to leave in the past those moments in life that are over."
— Paulo Coelho

"That is the nature of endings, it seems. They never end. When all the missing pieces of your life are found, put together with glue of memory and reason, there are more pieces to be found."
— Amy Tan

"We may run, walk, stumble. drive, or fly, but let us never lose sight of the reason for the journey, or miss a chance to see a rainbow on the way."
— Gloria Gaither

"The only journey is the one within." — Rainer Maria Rilke

"The greatest thing in this world is not so much where we stand as in what direction we are moving."
— Johann Wolfgang von Goethe

"Whole life is a search for beauty. But, when the beauty is found inside, the search ends and a beautiful journey begins."
— Harshit Walia

"The seeker embarks on a journey to find what he wants and discovers, along the way, what he needs."
— Wally Lamb

"The Sun will rise and set regardless. What we choose to do with the light while it's here is up to us. Journey wisely."
— Alexandra Elle

"The spiritual life does not remove us from the world
but moves us deeper into it." --Henry Nouwen

In every culture, religious and spiritual tradition the Creation stories support the underlying principles of the human understanding of the nature of the Divine and our connection with the Creator. Creation stories are part of the healing and nurturing of all of Creation itself. What images from this Creation story underpin your own ideas about life?

Genesis 1: 1-31 "In the beginning, God created the heavens and the earth. The earth was without form and void, and darkness was over the face of the deep. And the Spirit of God was hovering over the face of the waters. And God said, "Let there be light," and there was light. And God saw that the light was good. And God separated the light from the darkness. God called the light Day, and the darkness he called Night. And there was evening and there was morning, the first day. ..."

Throughout this retreat-in-daily life, we have been seeking a healing of our spiritual lives as we live out our daily experiences of life.

Spend some time today in celebration of your life, and of all the blessings and gifts you have. Spend some time honoring those who have come into or left you for each person who has been a part of our lives, has shared their gifts with us in some way. Take what you have gleaned from this experience, and weave it into your life as you continue to live out your purpose.

In our experience of life, we seek to communicate through our spiritual nature. The innate, Divine Presence that infuses all Creation animates and inspires us to our highest good. Our inner light and understanding is awakened through the use of our conscious and mindful awareness. As we become receptive and awakened to how the Universal flow of Light and healing energy is constantly flowing through us, we turn toward that unions of body, mind, Spirit, and soul, and receive what we need when we need it.
A retreat-in-daily life is an opportunity to turn toward the Presence of God within us, and to honor the daily lessons we are presented to open ourselves to the Truth within. As we open ourselves to the spiritual path before us, we discern the daily inpouring of inspiration, compassion, abundance, love, and affection we receive through the Holy Spirit. This beautiful awareness is a gift of grace. Through prayer and meditation we clear a path to receive, however, gifts of grace are ours through the Creator's Love and healing Presence. We have only to receive with open hearts, minds, and souls.

Inspirational Quotes.

"I understand once again that the greatness of God reveals itself in the simple things." Paolo Coehle

"We shall draw from the heart of suffering itself the means of inspiration and survival." -- Winston Churchill

"We have reached the top of the horizon, and have come toward the end of our journey. We stand on the threshold of pure thought, pure mind, and enlightenment. We have traveled from the depth of our physical selves, through the body, to the height of consciousness and have come to explore the soul of the Universe, the mind. Within each living creature is a brain, one that thinks, feels, and reacts. It comprises thousands of neurons and thousands of electromagnetic pulses that make up who we are...[our minds are like a thousand-petaled lotus] that represents and connects us to infinity. " --Czephyra Lunna, The Universal Mind

"The soil in which the meditative mind can begin is the soil of everyday life...in all this movement (life itself) you must somehow begin from the other end, from the other shore, and not always be concerned with this shore or how to cross the river. You must take the plunge into the water, not knowing how to swim. And the beauty of meditation is that you never know where you are, where you are going, what the end is." --Krisnamurti

"Your sacred space is where you find yourself over and over again." Joseph Campbell

"The first peace, which is the most important, is that which comes from within the souls of people when they realize their relationship, their oneness with the universe and all its powers, and when they realize at the center of the universe dwells the Great Spirit, and that its center is really everywhere, it is within each of us." Black Elk.

"Knock and He will open the door,
Vanish and He'll make you shine like the sun,
Fall and he will raise you to the heavens.
Become nothing and He'll turn you into everything." --Rumi

"Science is not only compatible with spirituality; it is a profound source of spirituality." --Carl Sagan

Each time you take time to do a retreat-in-daily life, also take some time to reflect on your experience. Fill a journal with your reflections and observations. Record your dreams and insights. Create something beautiful to express your feelings, experiences, and thoughts. Use this process to deepen your understanding of what it means to live a mindful life, ever aware of the series of thresholds that ask that we stop and consider what has been, what is calling us, and what we are preparing to enter. Blessings on your journey.

Notes from the Retreat-in-Daily Life:

Printed in Great Britain
by Amazon